INTRODUCTION

Of the many animal hobby pursuits you could involve yourself in, keeping fishes in an aquarium is undoubtedly one of the most fascinating and relaxing. Compared to other animal hobbies, such as the keeping of mammals or birds, aquarium fishkeeping is a relatively new pursuit, dating back only as far as the 19th Century. It is true that fishes had been kept by humans for many centuries prior to this, but these were maintained in outdoor ponds. Attempts to keep them in relatively small containers were always followed by disaster — the death of the fish in a short span of time.

Not until the chemistry of natural waters was understood could fishkeeping become a hobby. A British surgeon, Ellis, in *The Chemistry of Creation*, published in 1850, was one of the first scientists to document the importance of oxygen and carbon dioxide exchange in the fish/plant symbiosis. A chemist, Robert Warrington, studied the matter in more detail, and it was the English naturalist Philip Henry Gosse who first applied this knowledge in a practical manner.

Gosse built a number of vivariums (the original name applied to what is now an aquarium) and succeeded in maintaining a collection of both freshwater and saltwater fishes for a number of months. His research resulted in the opening of the world's first public

A red snakeskin produced in Singapore by Gan Aquarium Fish Farm.

PHOTO BY CHEW KENG LOON.

aquarium at the London Zoo in 1853. Other zoos, in Germany, France and elsewhere, followed suit and featured aquariums. The result was a great upsurge in public demand for information on the keeping of fishes. A new animal hobby was well and truly underway.

However, aquarists in those days were primitive by today's standards. Many millions of fishes died due to insufficient knowledge on the part of the owner—a fact that is still a reality in this hobby at the beginner level. In the early years most attention was directed toward freshwater fishes as home pets, the goldfish quickly establishing itself as the most popular species due to its very hardy and adaptable nature.

The availability of heaters, air pumps, and filters was a major step forward in technology, as it enabled species from warmer waters to be maintained successfully. This gave birth to the tropical fish hobby. It was to be the area of the hobby that would make the most rapid expansion, especially in the years following the end of World War II. Tropical fishes sport a greater array of colors and patterns than those from temperate climates. This alone ensured that they would remain perennial favorites ahead of those generally referred to as "coldwater" fishes, of which the ubiquitous goldfish was and remains the major focus of attention.

THE ARRIVAL OF THE GUPPY

Having given a brief historical backdrop to set the scene, we can now introduce the guppy, the

A blue snakeskin guppy produced by Gan Aquarium Fish Farm in Singapore.

PHOTO BY CHEW KENG LOON.

The famous Purple Dragon Head Guppy, so named by the Gan Aquarium Fish Farm who produced this fish. The popular names of guppy varieties are usually designated by the breeder who developed the strains. Often the same kind of fish has a different name in each of the international markets.

subject of this book. This tiny fish from South America is named for the English naturalist John Lechmere Guppy, who became incorrectly credited as being its discoverer. He took specimens from Trinidad to England, and the species was named *Girardinus guppyi* in his honor by Günther, the famed zoologist who was head of the British Museum at that time. (The genus *Girardinus* was named by Poey for the naturalist of the Smithsonian Institute, Charles Girard.) However, in 1863, before Guppy made his "discovery," the guppy had been collected and named *Lebistes poeciloides* by the Spaniard De Filippi. (*Lebistes* means "a kind of fish.") To complicate matters even further, the German zoologist J. L. Peters had collected the fish earlier still, in 1859, and named it

Poecilia reticulata (the latter meaning "net-like"). In 1913 the guppy was called *Lebistes reticulatus* by Regan. This was generally accepted until quite recent times, although other names were in use. Today, the name given by Peters back in 1859 takes priority.

Although guppies were imported into Europe and the USA during the latter part of the 19th century, it was not until the 1920s that they started to gain popularity as pets. Indeed, even then there was only limited interest in them. This persisted until about the late 1950s, when concerted efforts there were to selectively breed color variants.

As with any pet, when mutations start to appear there is invariably an explosion of interest in the species. This was very much the case with these tiny fish. During the next two decades they really became fashionable. By the late 1970s there was already an extensive range of colors and fin types, and the development of the guppy has continued to this day. Today, no other fish, including the many gorgeous koi, can rival them in this area. Of all pets, probably only the budgerigar as a single species enjoys a comparable following of dedicated breeders.

THE BASIS OF THE GUPPY'S SUCCESS

Clearly, the multitude of colors, their patterns, and fin shapes, have been the cornerstone on which the guppy's success has been built. But these are by no means the only sources of its

appeal; it has many other virtues. The guppy is an excellent community fish, being non-aggressive toward other species. It is arguably the hardiest of all tropical fishes in that it will survive in a range of water temperatures and conditions that few other species, other than perhaps the goldfish, could tolerate. It is a very willing breeder, so much so that if both sexes are present you would find it impossible to stop them from breeding!

Its size is yet another major plus for it as an aquarium fish. You can keep a large number of guppies in a relatively small tank and thus have a magnificent display for a very low financial outlay. It must also be stated that some breeders keep guppies

A wild guppy male.

PHOTO BY MP & C PIEDNOIR, AQUAPRESS.

PHOTO BY CHEW KENG LOON.

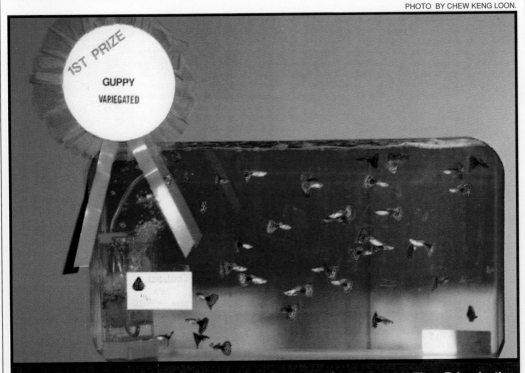

This tank filled with variegated guppies, all almost identical, won First Prize in the Variegated Guppy Class at the Aquarium Show held in Singapore in 1993.

purely as feeder species for carnivorous fishes. But we are interested only in having them as piscine jewels in their own right.

You really could not begin in this hobby with a better fish, whether you keep them with other species in a community tank, as the focus of your entire display, or as "moving ornaments" for an aquarium that is primarily a display of live plants.

Although guppies are as undemanding a species as you could find, nonetheless they cannot be abused if they are to be healthy and impressive aquarium occupants. Likewise, if breeding is to be undertaken, it is important that you take this very seriously; otherwise, you will soon become disenchanted in the steady deterioration that will ensue if carefully planned breeding is not the order of the day. In the following chapters is all the basic information you need to know.

WHAT IS A GUPPY?

You do not need to have the knowledge of an ichthyologist in order to maintain and breed guppies successfully. But a basic understanding of what a guppy is all about will be useful. If you are a first-time aquarist you should also understand a little about the ways fishes are broadly grouped in hobby circles.

WHERE FISHES LIVE

Over 70% of the earth's surface is covered by water, most of it by large seas and oceans that are rich in salts. This latter fact has a considerable bearing on the types of water fishes have evolved to live in. This provides our first major division of fishes from a hobby viewpoint: marine and freshwater. The guppy is one of the latter.

Marine fishes live in an environment that has a greater

Freshwater fishes have the reverse problem. Their body fluids are denser than the water they live in, and water constantly diffuses into their bodies. Thus, they drink little, if at all, while releasing large amounts of urine. In actual fact, the guppy, like the goldfish, is capable of living in

PHOTO BY CHEW KENG LOON.

The fabled Green Diamond Guppy developed by Gan Aquarium Fish Farm in Singapore.

density than the fluids in the fish's body. Via a process known as *osmosis*, marine fishes are constantly losing water to the surrounding environment, so must drink copious amounts of it in order to remain at equilibrium. These fishes also release minimal fecal matter, and that which is excreted is high in salts. Excess salts that marine fishes gain when they drink seawater is actively pumped out through cells in the gill filaments.

mildly saline waters that would kill many freshwater fishes. But for all practical purposes you should regard this species as a freshwater fish.

You may astutely be aware that eels, salmon, and sticklebacks, to name but three species, move from one type of water to the other during certain periods of their lives. (These fishes are called *diadromous*.) They have very specialized kidneys and other physiological modifications that enable them to do this.

The inability of most freshwater fishes to survive in salt water has an important side effect when it comes to eradicating parasites and other pathogens. This is worthy of mention. Most parasites also have evolved to live in either fresh or salt water, but not both. If they are subjected to waters not conducive to their metabolism, it always near freezing, while in the tropics it usually is warm. (However, the depth of the water, the elevation, and the speed at which it is flowing also will affect temperature.) Temperature gives us the second major division within the aquatic hobby, tropical vs. temperate, but this parameter is much more flexible than is

The blue variegated snakeskin guppy produced by Gan Aquarium Fish Farm.

will effect their ability to regulate their water content. Their body cells will either swell excessively and literally burst, or implode due to excessive loss of fluid. This is why short-term saltwater baths are very effective in the treatment of some parasite problems in freshwater fishes.

THE TEMPERATURE FACTOR

There is a considerable range in the temperature of waters found on Earth. In polar regions it is tolerance to salinity.

There are coldwater species, such as the goldfish, and tropical fishes, the guppy being one of the latter. However, the guppy has the ability to survive in cooler waters that would certainly kill most tropical fishes. It is this ability to withstand a wide range of conditions, which includes water hardness and pH values, that makes the guppy one of the most adaptable of fishes.

This does not mean that

guppies should be subjected to sudden changes or steady abuse of their water conditions. It means that as a species they have the ability to adapt to a range of conditions if these are introduced slowly and thereafter remain constant.

It should also be noted that inbred strains, especially those that show considerable divergence in form and color from the wild type, are far less able to withstand change. The reason that this is so lies in the fact that the mutations that create these beautiful strains and individuals may bring with them minor physiological changes. These affect membrane permeability and gill function, as well as other aspects of metabolism. Taken together, they make the individual less able to adapt than the wild types, and thus more vulnerable to changes in their watery world.

METHODS OF REPRODUCTION

Apart from dividing fishes into groups based on the salinity of the water and its temperature, hobbyists also distinguish between the way fishes reproduce. Those fishes (the majority) that lay eggs that hatch outside of the female's body are called egglayers, the technical term being *oviparous*. This is a rather wasteful method of reproduction because most of the eggs will quickly be eaten or perish in other ways.

Some evolutionarily recent fishes developed ways to reduce the number of eggs needed and ensuring that a greater percentage of young would survive. Although other strategies are used by fishes, livebearing is a

This purple guppy was a true strain perfected and marketed by Gan Aquarium Fish Farm in Singapore.

PHOTO BY CHEW KENG LOON.

This magnificent green guppy with a solid yellow tail was given the strain name Yellowtail by Gan Aquarium Fish Farm, the producer of this fish.

major one. Livebearing species, of which the guppy is one, retain the eggs in the female's body until they have hatched. They live off the small yolks of the eggs but also get some nourishment directly from the mother. The fry are born as diminutive replicas of their parents. Only about 500 or so of the 20,000-plus fish species are included within this group, but they are among the most popular of aquarium fishes. Livebearers also include the mollies, platies, swordtails, goodeids, and a few odds and ends.

Livebearers are of two types. In one, the eggs are merely retained within the ovaries or oviduct and develop mainly from nutrients derived from the yolk included in their yolk sac. These are called *ovoviviparous*. In the other type, the embryos are nourished by the female via placenta-like structures; these are the "true" livebearers, or *viviparous* fishes. The guppy is usually said to be ovoviviparous; however, as we noted, there definitely is some maternal contribution to the nourishment of the embryos, so you will appreciate that the distinction between the two methods is not a clear-cut line.

In order to deposit sperm into the female, the livebearers had to develop a sort of penis. This was achieved by modifying part of the anal fin into a copulatory organ known as a *gonopodium*. When breeding, the gonopodium of the guppy is rotated forward and usually to one side. It forms a tube for the passage of packets of sperm (*spermatophores*) into the oviduct of the female so that they can fertilize the ripe eggs in the ovaries.

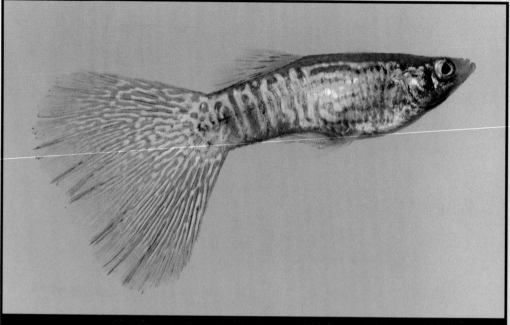

A golden snakeskin guppy produced by Gan Aquarium Fish Farm. Gan exports to markets all over the world and might well be the world's largest producer of both guppies and discus.

Female guppies have the ability to store some of these "packets" in the ovaries so that they can be used to fertilize eggs at a latter date. This adaptation is seen in all poeciliids. If you were not aware of this ability you would be surprised if you obtained some female guppies and noted that they produced offspring in the absence of a male. Guppies are not hermaphroditic (both sex organs in the same individual), or parthenogenetic (capable of reproduction without the need for a male to fertilize the eggs).

THE GUPPY: A DESCRIPTION

With a basic understanding of where the guppy fits into the aquarium hobby, we can now focus more closely on it as an individual species.

Distribution: The original distribution of the guppy is northeastern South America (Brazil to Venezuela) and the islands of Trinidad, Barbados, and others nearby. It has been introduced into many countries, both tropical and temperate, in order to help eradicate mosquito larvae. Thus, its distribution in the tropics is now pretty much cosmopolitan.

Habitat: The guppy is found in shallow rivers, streams, lakes, lagoons, and estuaries where the water may be fresh or brackish.

Size: The female is larger, reaching 2.4 inches (6 cm); the male grows to 1.4 inches (3.5 cm).

Color: The basic wild-type color pattern is very variable, but comprises silver, green, brown, blue, red, and black. The females are much more somber in coloration than the males, though through selective breeding they have become more appealing. By the same process, the very ordinary-looking male wild guppy has become a piscine jewel that can sport a whole rainbow of colors.

Fins: The guppy sports typical fish finnage in that it has single dorsal, caudal (tail), and anal fins, plus paired pectoral and pelvic (ventral) fins. The dorsal is short and begins just behind the midline of the body. The paired pelvics are situated well behind the pectorals, but anterior to the dorsal, and just forward of the anal. The latter has been modified in the male to form the gonopodium already discussed.

The dorsal and caudal fins display tremendous variation in domestic guppies, where, through selective breeding of mutations, they have become both larger and quite variable in shape.

Mouth: The mouth is terminal and superior. This latter term means its opens dorsally and indicates that the guppy generally is a surface feeder, which of course is where it would snatch mosquito larvae, small insects, and similar prey. The mouth features membranous lips that are well supplied with sensory nerve endings.

Other Anatomical Features: The guppy is a very typical fish in that its body is covered with scales, it has a two-chambered heart, kidneys, and other organs found in all vertebrate animals. One organ, the gas or swim bladder, is

The green snakeskin guppy bred by Gan Aquarium Fish Farm in Singapore.

PHOTO BY CHEW KENG LOON.

Not every strain is a winner. This Ocelot Guppy developed by Gan wasn't a financial success.

worthy of comment. This organ is useful to many fishes because it acts as a hydrostatic mechanism that enables the fish to move between different water depths, or to remain motionless at a given depth without expending undue amounts of energy. Fish flesh is denser than water, so the fish achieves neutral buoyancy by adjusting the amount of gases in the bladder, thus changing the overall density of its body. As the gases are reduced the density increases and the fish will start to sink; as the bladder is filled the density drops and the fish will rise. The fish increases or reduces the gaseous content of its swim bladder by the secretion or absorption of gases directly from or to the blood.

If you would like to learn more about the anatomy and physiology of fishes, your pet shop should have some good general books on ichthyology.

This magnificent variegated lower swordtail guppy was produced and photographed by Tanaka in Japan.

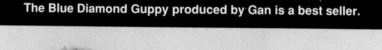

The Blue Diamond Guppy produced by Gan is a best seller.

UNDERSTANDING WATER QUALITY

You undoubtedly are aware that water can have many tastes or flavors depending on its source. In part, such tastes are created by the minerals and chemicals from the natural environment, as well as those that may or may not have been added to it to make it safe to drink. The amounts of gases (oxygen, carbon dioxide, ammonia, etc.) also are important. If water flows over rocks that are rich in calcium and other soft minerals it will be hard and usually alkaline. If it flows over land that contains much organic material it will be acidic and usually soft.

The temperature of a body of water (such as that in your aquarium) will have an influence over the amount of oxygen it can contain. The warmer it is, the less dissolved oxygen it can hold. This, in turn, affects the number of fishes that can be accommodated. However, more important is the surface area of the water, because it is at this interface that oxygen enters the water and carbon dioxide and other gases leave. The greater the surface area, the greater the amount of oxygen that can be dissolved. The smaller the area, the less oxygen that can be held, almost regardless of the depth.

The cleanliness of the water is a significant factor in fishkeeping success. Uneaten food, the decaying leaves of plants, fecal matter from fishes, and other organic matter will all tend to produce levels of ammonia, nitrites, phosphates and other compounds that can be lethal to your fishes, i.e., beyond their levels of tolerance. They will not only affect the oxygen and carbon dioxide content of the water, but they will also negatively affect the mucus layer that protects the fish's skin. Once this is impaired, parasites and other pathogens (disease-causing organisms) may attack the fish. Very soon it will be unhealthy and make the water even more dangerous for other fishes by exposing them to high levels of pathogens.

Natural waters retain their ecological stability—be this very fresh and clean, somewhat dirty, brackish, hard, acidic, and so on— by the forces of nature they are subject to. Winds, rain, the ever-moving nature of water, its considerable volume, the migratory nature of some fishes (even if over a small distance) and the plants and other organisms (large predators to microscopic animals) in the water, all help to create a natural balance to which all its life forms have adapted.

But in the aquarium these forces are not present. Unless you continually compensate for them with sound husbandry, the water quality will rapidly degenerate. Controlling water quality at a level that is acceptable to all the inhabitants of a system is a big part of what the hobby is all about.

This does not mean you must be forever checking the pH or other values, for over-attention can sometimes be as detrimental as a lack of it. A common-sense approach that combines a keen sense of observation of conditions, and of the fish, is more important than meddling with conditions when this would be inappropriate. Consistency of routine is what you should aim for. With the help of mechanical aids (filters, etc.) it is now possible to maintain virtually any type of water so that it remains clean and largely free from contaminants and unwanted organisms.

What you must remember is that when you first set up an aquarium the water is by no means "mature" enough to maintain a collection of guppies. It must be carefully prepared so that vital biological processes can begin. You also must monitor pH, hardness, and temperature, to be sure they are suited to the species, in this case guppies, that are to live in that water.

The wise aquarist will therefore prepare the aquarium at least two or more weeks before the fish are introduced. When the water quality appears to be stabilized at the required levels, only then should a few guppies be introduced. The aquarium still requires more weeks to further mature after the initial fish are added. Thereafter, additional stock can only be accommodated on a gradual basis.

An aquarium may be compared to a fine wine. You cannot rush its maturation, in spite of the additives that can help these days, you must allow this to happen on a gradual basis for the very best results.

pH

The pH of water is a measure of its acidity or alkalinity. A scale of 0-14 is used, where 7.0 is the neutral point. Below this is acidic, the more so as you approach 0. Above 7.0 is alkaline. A movement of 1.0 up or down the scale represents a tenfold increase in acidity or alkalinity; for example, water with a pH of 6.0 is ten times more acidic than water of 7.0.

Every aquarist must have the ability to test the quality of the aquarium water. Water test kits are available at most pet shops.

The guppy is best kept within the range of pH 6.8-7.4. Fortunately, this is a range into which domestic tap water frequently falls. The pH will fluctuate depending on temperature, type of gravel used, oxygen content, uneaten foods, and other organic debris created. It is best to test the water at the same time of day when monitoring regularly, so that 24-hour fluctuations do not give you what might appear to be incorrect readings.

Test kits are stocked by your pet shop and come complete with all instructions. There are various types which use either a liquid reagent, powder, or tablets. There are also several models of electronic pH monitors, but these are expensive, though very accurate and easy to use. Make sure that any test kit or monitor you obtain will measure in the 6.0-7.6 range, which encompasses our target range for guppies.

AMMONIA (NH$_3$)

This is a gas that is very soluble in water and is produced by fishes as a waste product, as well as by the bacterial breakdown of organic matter in the aquarium.

Beyond 0.2 mg per liter (possibly even a little lower) it may be lethal to your fish. Eventually, beneficial bacteria will grow in your filter and gravel that will convert the ammonia to nitrite (NO$_2$). Nitrite is still dangerous, but a little less so than ammonia—0.5 mg/liter is the lethal point. The good news is that other bacteria convert the nitrite to nitrate (NO$_3$), which is relatively safe up to 100 mg/liter. These chemical processes are called the *nitrogen cycle* (because all the compounds contain nitrogen), and the bacterial processes that convert ammonia to nitrite to nitrate are the basis of *biological filtration.*

Ammonia toxicity is linked to pH: in water that has a pH below 7.0, the effects of ammonia are reduced, while in alkaline water they are sharply amplified. Test kits are available for ammonia, nitrite, and nitrate, but the interrelationship of these chemicals in the nitrogen cycle is such that for all practical purposes only one is needed. That for nitrites is suggested. If nitrites are low, it means the nitrogen cycle is functional and ammonia is being converted to nitrite and then to nitrate.

It is worth mentioning that many beginners mistake nitrite poisoning for oxygen starvation in newly set-up tanks simply because they see the fishes gasping at the surface. This is a common reaction of fishes to many different toxins because toxins damage gill tissues, so the fishes try to breathe the oxygen-rich air right at the surface. This is why it is so important to test for nitrite.

WATER HARDNESS

The amount of salts in the water makes the water hard or soft. When you boil a kettle of hard water, you are no doubt aware of the lime that forms. The same is true of lime that builds up in domestic water heaters and pipes. Fishes have evolved to live in waters within given hard or soft water ranges. If these are not supplied their gills, fins, and internal organs will be negatively effected, and breeding results will suffer badly as well.

Hardness is measured in numerous ways, but the two most popular methods are parts per million (ppm) of calcium carbonate ($CaCO_3$), or degrees of hardness (dH), which indicate the parts of calcium oxide (CaO) per 100,000 parts of water.

Understanding the chemistry of hardness is complex, but using one of the available test kits makes things simple for you.

The guppy is best suited to hardness in the range of dH 10-30°, which is equal to 180-540 ppm. This translates to water that is medium to hard, with a dH of 12-18° possibly being the preferred state.

CHLORINE & CHLORAMINE

Chlorine is a gas that readily dissolves in water, and which has a destructive effect on the respiratory tract. It is easily dissipated into the atmosphere if water is allowed to stand for 24 hours, or if it is vigorously stirred. Chloramines are compounds of chlorine and ammonia that are much more stable than chlorine gas, so are not as easily removed from water. Both are added to domestic water supplies in order to kill pathogens, so must be removed before fishes are introduced. Test kits are produced for chlorine and chloramine. Your pet shop will

The Blond Diamond Guppy produced in Singapore by Gan Aquarium Fish Farm.

PHOTO BY CHEW KENG LOON.

A wonderful blue variegated guppy with a black body. The fish was produced at Gan Aquarium Fish Farm in Singapore.

also have chemicals designed to neutralize chlorine and chloramines.

OTHER CHEMICALS IN THE WATER

Although the number of other chemicals in water is many, one or two should be mentioned. Copper is a potentially lethal element for fishes beyond certain tolerances. For this reason, it is always wise to run a faucet for 30 seconds before using the water. This removes copper or metals that may be in your tap water from your pipes.

Phosphate is another chemical compound that should be tested for if the water is suffering from algal bloom (an excess of algal growth that turns the water green).

You also can obtain dissolved oxygen and carbon dioxide test kits, but these normally are unnecessary for the guppy hobbyist.

ADJUSTING WATER PROPERTIES

There are numerous ways in which you can adjust the properties of the water until it is satisfactory for your needs. Your pet shop sells a wide range of water conditioners for different purposes, such as removing chlorine, copper, and other gases, metals or compounds. Filtration will also help in this direction, as discussed in the next chapter.

Hardness and pH can be adjusted by adding or removing

calcareous rocks and gravel, and by the addition of specific resins, or aquarium peat. The addition of acids directly to established tanks to lower pH is not advised and should be done (if at all) in water prepared before it is added to the tank. You can also reduce alkalinity and hardness by dilution with rain or distilled water until the required levels are established.

DOMESTIC WATER

The water you obtain from your tap is the most convenient way in which to supply your aquarium. However, because it is treated with so many chemicals it cannot be used as is: it must be prepared before using it for the fishes. Furthermore, do not assume that any readings you have obtained from your domestic supply are valid months, or even weeks, later. Following heavy rains or flooding, water authorities will increase the amount of this or that chemical to reinforce hygiene. This can cause havoc for the less-than-diligent aquarists who assume that their tap water is of a constant quality.

WATER CHANGES

As we noted earlier, buildups of wastes and other organic matter occur in the aquarium. In order to avoid the risk of chemical saturation to a potentially lethal level, it is wise to make regular partial water changes. In addition to diluting wastes and other chemicals, water changes may reduce some of the pathogens that are ever-present in any tank. It also

A magnificent golden snakeskin guppy produced by Gan Aquarium Fish Farm.

PHOTO BY CHEW KENG LOON.

has a tonic effect on the fish. Hobbyists differ considerably as to how often and how much water should be changed. A general guide would be about 20% every two weeks (taken from the lower levels, where the most pollutants will be), but the size of the aquarium, the number of fish and plants, as well as the extent of detritus that is observed, will all influence this decision. With guppies, it is safe to say that you should change as much water as you can, as often as you can.

When making water changes you must of course ensure that the new water is of the correct temperature.

Gan took first prize in the variegated guppy classification at an Aquarama Guppy Show held in Singapore.

Regular partial water changes are a necessity for your guppies' health. These changes can be made without siphons and buckets by using a labor saving automatic water changer.

A difference of one or two degrees will not harm the fish, but larger fluctuations could induce stress and shock, which obviously are undesirable. Likewise, you must ensure that there are no sudden changes to the pH and hardness. Always remember that most fishes can adjust to slow changes in their environment, but those that are abrupt will be deleterious to their health.

When first reading about water quality and some of the equipment for measuring and treating it, you may think that the hobby will be difficult for you. This will not be so—things will quickly fall into place. What is important is that you do not rush into stocking a new tank and by so doing place the lives of the fish at risk simply because water conditions were not carefully prepared.

By taking your time in ensuring that the water has matured, you not only gain practical knowledge, but can make mistakes without having them prove too costly.

THE TANK AND ITS EQUIPMENT

The first thing you should be aware of is that bigger is most definitely better when it comes to selecting an aquarium. Furthermore, a simple, old-fashioned rectangular tank is superior to fancy designs that are tall, round, or in other ways fashioned with esthetics rather than practicality in mind.

The advantages that large tank sizes provide are numerous: 1) They retain stable water quality more readily. As a result, routine maintenance is reduced. 2) They retain their temperature better. In the event of a short-duration power loss they will not lose heat as quickly as smaller tanks. On a water-volume to heat-cost basis they are more economic than smaller units. 3) Their extra space provides for more interesting aquascaping, and for concealing in-tank equipment such as filters and air lines. 4) They will accommodate more fish. 5) They are more impressive from an esthetic standpoint.

The foregoing comments are applicable to a typical home display tank. Breeders will use smaller units for breeding their guppies, as well as for hospitalization and quarantine purposes. You will appreciate that the more costly units will generally have a longer service life, and probably will be made using superior glass. As a general guide, a tank of 15-30 gallons will do nicely for most needs of the casual guppy hobbyist. If you prefer (and can afford) a more impressive unit, a larger tank can be selected. However, do bear in mind that water is very heavy, so you should make sure that the spot you've chosen can support the weight of the filled tank.

The following information will enable you to calculate volume and weight data for any tank.

Volume = Length x Width x Height

3,785 cubic cm = 1 US gallon

231 cubic in = 1 US gallon

1 Imperial (UK) gallon = 1.2 US gallons = 4.55 Liters

1 US Gallon = 0.833 UK gallons = 3.785 Liters

1 US gallon weighs 8.345lb (3.8kg)

1 UK gallon weighs 10lb (4.55kg)

1 Liter weighs 1kg or 2.2lb

1 Liter = 61cu.in or 1,000 cu. cm

Surface area = Length x width

When selecting your aquarium, do purchase one that comes complete with a full hood with lights. This reduces heat loss and water loss through evaporation.

STOCKING LEVELS

There are many factors that will determine the potential maximum stocking level of an aquarium. Among these are: 1) The water temperature. The cooler it is, the more oxygen it can contain. 2) Its

PHOTO BY AQUA PRESS, MC & P. PIEDNOIR.

Singapore and Japan produce lovely guppies, but Europe and the USA produce magnificent guppies as well. This is a tank filled with golden snakeskins. They all look very much alike and this is the objective of most guppy breeding programs.

cleanliness. Dirty water will hold less oxygen than clean water. 3) The bulk of the fish (its girth). The greater this is, the greater the fish's oxygen consumption. 4) The activity level of the fish. The more active it is, the more oxygen it requires. (Temperature also will influence activity level). 5) The extent of plantings. Live plants consume oxygen during night hours, though it is not a major factor. 6) The chemical composition of the water. This will affect both the amount of oxygen that can be held, as well as the activity and respiratory rate of the fish. 7) The surface area of the water. Oxygen is dissolved into water at the water/atmosphere interface. For practical purposes, the depth of the water is of little consequence. It provides for more space for the fish and plants, and will affect the amount of light that

will reach the lower levels. In very tall tanks it will produce temperature stratification in the absence of ancillary equipment to create circulation.

Clearly, the complexity of these various factors could make stocking level calculations a nightmare. Fortunately, aquarists have established a rule of thumb that works well enough to be a useful guide. It is that a typical tank that is maintained correctly, and without the need for additional equipment, can be stocked at the rate of one inch (2.5cm) of fish (not including the tail) per gallon of water, or one inch of fish or for every 12 square inches (78 square cm) of surface area.

As an example, a tank 24 x 12 x 12in (60 x 30 x 30cm) has a surface area of 288 square inches (1890 square cm). This means it

Green double swordtail guppy produced by Gan Aquarium Fish Farm.

PHOTO BY CHEW KENG LOON.

PHOTO BY CHEW KENG LOON.

Gan's interpretation of a ribbon tail guppy.

can accommodate 24 in (60cm) of fish. If the average guppy length (male-female mix) is 1.5 in (3.8 cm), the stocking level is 16 fish. You must bear in mind that if you base the number on juveniles you will be able to stock more fish—but as they mature you will have overstocked the aquarium.

The stocking level quoted may not seem very high and is worthy of further comment. It assumes a tank is not fitted with auxiliary equipment, and is a natural biological entity (which can never really be the case) in which only partial water changes are made. In reality, stocking levels can be considerably increased if we can increase the oxygen content of the water, and remove the higher quantities of fecal matter and other toxins.

This can be achieved with aeration and filtration equipment. What must be considered is that if these should fail to operate for any reason (breakdown or power loss), conditions in the tank will rapidly deteriorate, the more so the smaller the aquarium, and major problems will quickly result.

The wise aquarist will therefore never risk excessive stocking of a tank simply because the equipment makes this possible. A balanced judgment is the answer, in which a few extra fish are included, but not so many as might create stress, bullying, and pushing the filter system to overload potential.

AERATION

The object of aeration is to disturb the water surface by passing air through one or more diffuser stones attached to a tube connected to a small air pump. The result is a stream of bubbles that rise and burst at the surface.

It is the effect of this bursting that creates miniature waves, and these effectively increase the surface area of the water so it can take up more oxygen.

This stated, we can now consider a basic misconception about these bubbles. Little if any oxygen is absorbed into the water from the bubbles themselves. It is their effect on the surface area that is the all-important factor. As the bubbles rise they also have a secondary effect. They draw water up behind them in the partial vacuum they create. Thus, they help to take unwanted gases to the surface, and help in creating circulation of the water, which is further aided by the use of one or more heaters.

The bubble size is of some importance. If it is too large it rises too quickly to draw water behind it all they way to the top, if it is too small, it does not hold sufficient air to disturb the surface enough to provide maximum aeration, nor does it provide maximum circulation. Some experimentation is always needed to obtain a satisfactory balance.

Simple aeration can almost double the stocking capacity of an aquarium. It can also be used to create esthetic appeal. Ceramic diffuser stones are the preferred choice. These can be small or large in order to create single or multiple columns of bubbles. They can be discretely hidden at the back of the tank, or placed into an ornament.

There are two types of pumps you can choose from. One is the diaphragm type; the other works by piston action. The former is the cheaper and most popular. It should be sited above the tank (to remove the risk of back-siphoning in the event of a power outage) either suspended or placed on a non-slip surface; otherwise, it will tend to "skate" around and cause noise. Pumps come in a number of sizes, depending on how much air is provided. The airflow can be controlled by a knob on some models, or by clamps or valves on the connected air line(s).

FILTRATION

If an efficient filter system is part of your setup, it removes the need for a separate aerator because it can perform this function itself. The filter can be of the foam, canister, box, undergravel, or wheel type, the lattermost being the latest concept. So, there are lots of choices, each offering its own advantages in efficiency, size, or cost.

Rather than discuss the merits of various filter types, it is better that you understand how filtration is achieved. You can then discuss your particular needs with your pet shop personnel. The objects of filtration are: 1) To remove large unwanted materials in suspension, such as uneaten food, fecal matter, and the like. 2) To remove dangerous gases, such as ammonia. 3) To remove dangerous compounds, such as nitrites, or to create an environment in which beneficial bacteria will convert them to nitrates that can be used as a food by plants. 4) To remove various unidentified compounds that may either "color" the water, or that may be harmful to the fish. 5) To remove any residual medicines that may from time to time be used in the aquarium.

Removal is achieved in one of three ways: 1) Mechanical: The

In reality, the three methods may overlap. For example, a mechanical filter using foam or gravel will provide a surface for beneficial bacteria to live on, as will zeolite, which is essentially a chemical filter. Live plants act in all three capacities, while the aquarium substrate provides mechanical and biological filtration.

A Gan tuxedo Guppy.

water is passed through a material, such as foam or polyester floss, that effectively blocks the passage of solids. 2) Chemical: The water is passed through a medium, such as charcoal or zeolite, which absorbs gases and other chemicals. 3) Biological: The water is passed over a medium rich in beneficial bacteria that convert ammonia and nitrites into the less dangerous nitrates, which are utilized by plants as fertilizer.

However, biological filtration can only be achieved if the water surrounding the medium is rich in oxygen, because the bacteria are *aerobic*, meaning they utilize oxygen for their chemical processing.

Whatever filtration system is used, the water can be returned to the surface so that it agitates this, thus aerating it. It can be returned via a spray bar, which increases the aeration because the water is exposed to the atmosphere as it falls onto the surface.

However, guppies are native to relatively slow-moving waters, so excessive water movement is not essential. Filters should be so arranged that they draw the water from just above the substrate, where it will be the dirtiest and least-aerated.

It is essential that whatever system is used it must be maintained on a regular basis, otherwise the filter will become clogged and ineffective, indeed dangerous. Partial water changes are still needed regardless of how good the filter system is.

HEATING

Guppies prefer a temperature in the range of 72-78°F (22-26°C), though they can cope with variables above or below this. The important thing about heat is that it should be constant, not fluctuating, which rapidly induces stress and chills, thus leading to more serious ailments.

A rule-of-thumb guide to the heater capacity is 5 watts per gallon. A 15-gallon tank will therefore need a 75-watt heater. This assumes a typical home environment. If the tank is large, say, 40 gallons or larger, the watts per gallon can be reduced to about 3.5, because the larger water volume is able to retain its heat much better than a smaller volume.

In very large tanks it is wise to use two heaters whose combined wattage is as desired, or a little above this. It avoids the possibility that if a heater fails the temperature will fall dramatically; you always have a backup. Do not

A blond tuxedo guppy developed by Gan Aquarium Fish Farm.

PHOTO BY CHEW KENG LOON.

Two male Gan Tuxedo's developed at the Gan Aquarium Fish Farm in Singapore.

use a heater that is too powerful for the volume of water to be heated. If the thermostat should stick in the "on" position the heater may take the temperature way above normal, and before you notice the problem it may "cook" the fish!

Heaters are available in a range of types, but the most popular are the combined heater/thermostat submersibles that feature a temperature dial and a pilot light. As a back-up indicator that the water temperature is as required, you should have a thermometer placed at the opposite end of the aquarium from the heater. This should be checked daily as a matter of routine. Your pet shop stocks a range of models. It is prudent to always keep a spare heater on hand.

LIGHTING

Light is required for your aquarium to achieve two major biological functions, plus those that are esthetic. It is vital for plant growth and for the general well-being of the fish, whose feeding and swimming activities are determined by light/dark cycles. If overhead artificial light is not included the fish may start to swim at an angle, and plants may grow toward the direction of whatever light there is (usually daylight entering the front of the tank). The type and intensity of artificial light used will greatly influence the appearance of colors.

The desired light/dark cycle is 12 hours, which approximates the cycle found in tropical regions. With regard to the wattage required, general guide lines are as follows (using fluorescent lighting):

Tank Length Method: 10 watts for every 12 in (30cm) of length.

Surface Area Method: 10 watts for every 140 square inches (900 square cm).

Volume Method: 1.5 watts per gallon if the tank is of rectangular size and a depth comparable with the width.

With regard to the type of lighting needed, you will need to experiment a little to find the one that best suits your plants. There are those that have a bias towards the red or blue end of the spectrum, and are best for plants. These will also enhance certain of the guppy's colors, while creating a rather false impression of others. Conversely, natural daylight tubes, which highlight the natural color of your fish, are not quite as good for plant growth. In a larger tank you use one of each, but for smaller ones you may have to choose one or the other.

There are very many variables that can affect both heat and light requirements. These are subjects you should delve further into. There are many good books available at your local pet shop.

A lovely variegatd blue snakeskin guppy developed by Gan Aquarium Fish Farm.

SETTING UP A DISPLAY TANK

Before you begin setting up your display tank, again, consider its site with care. Avoid placing it where it may be subjected to drafts—such as opposite doors. Likewise, it should not be so placed that it will receive long hours of direct sunlight. Apart from the risk of overheating, the rays of the sun may encourage strong algal growth at the front and sides of the tank.

THE SUBSTRATE

To provide both a pleasing look and a good surface for beneficial bacteria to live on, a substrate of gravel is required. This should be neither too large nor too small. The latter packs tightly and does not allow for large bacterial colonization or for plant roots, while the former provides too many spaces for uneaten food and debris to collect. A particle size in the range of 2-3 mm is about right.

Avoid using any material containing calcium and magnesium carbonates, as these will make the water too alkaline. Examples are chalk, dolomite, marble, and coral. The best gravel and rocks are granite, slate, sandstone, and similar hard rocks that are chemically neutral in water, thus not affecting its composition. You should obtain your gravel and rocks from pet shops only, but even these should be routinely washed a number of times before being used. This will remove any dust and debris that

would otherwise cloud the water. Careful cleaning of everything placed into your aquarium should become your normal routine. It really does reduce the risk of introducing toxins or pathogens into the water.

DECORATIONS

Among the many items that can be used for decorating your display are bogwood and driftwood, roots, cork (weighted), bamboo, and any of the many excellent synthetic rocks, wood, and plants now produced for aquarists. All of these will take on a more natural look as they become covered with algae, on which the fish will browse. Avoid jagged rocks.

Aquarists fall into two broad types. There are those who try to create a very natural look to their aquascape, even though it may not be a faithful reproduction of the habitat of the fishes they keep. There are also those who enjoy novelty effects using colored gravel, sunken ships, and ruins of bygone civilizations. Beauty is in the eye of the beholder, so whatever maintains your interest in the hobby is quite acceptable.

PLANTS

A number of roles are played by plants in an aquarium. Foremost to most aquarists is their beauty—the range of greens, reds, and blue-browns they can

Decorative items to be used in an aquarium should be designed specifically for use in an aquarium. Many products are toxic and poison the tank by slowly releasing toxins into the water. Only use ornaments you buy at your local aquarium shop.

produce is matched only by the considerable variety of their leaf shapes and growth habits. But they serve an important biological function in helping to keep the water healthy. They remove nitrates, various salts, and a number of other elements and compounds from the water.

They provide sheltered spots for the fish to rest in, as well as refuge for small fry, or from other fishes if these are kept in a community tank alongside the peaceful guppies. Finally, they are a source of food for the guppies, who will browse on the algae they attract, as well as on the microorganisms that live on them.

Of course, you can purchase many synthetic plants that will serve most of these functions, although they will not be chemical and biological filters. Many hobbyists combine living plants with artificial plants, and to very good effect. What you must always appreciate is that plants are as demanding as the fish are of appropriate water conditions. They have evolved to live in certain waters—acidic, alkaline, hard or soft, and at preferred temperatures, just like your guppies. Indeed, many plants will be more demanding of water conditions than will the fish. Some are very hardy, others extremely delicate. Some like bright lighting; others softer, more diffused light. Each of these needs must be taken into account before they are purchased.

When choosing plants it is best to select only a few and make a good display of these rather than to try to establish a botanical garden of species in your aquarium. Select shorter plants for the foreground, larger ones for the sides and rear of the aquarium. Avoid making things too formal and symmetrical. Large rocks and driftwood placed off-center are much more pleasing on the eye than if they occupy center stage.

You will probably find that certain plants regarded as difficult or easy to establish by some aquarists may not be so in your aquarium. This comment holds true for fishes and many other animals as well, meaning that you must experiment to find the ones that thrive for you and the conditions you have created in your mini-ecosystem.

Your pet shop can advise you as to which plants are best suited to your needs. At the same time, you are advised to research more on plants with respect to their requirements and methods of propagation.

USEFUL TOOLS

The final things you will need before you are ready to set up your display do not cost much, but will be needed time and again. These include a length of plastic piping for siphoning purposes, one or two scrapers for cleaning the aquarium glass, one or two 3- to 5-gallon plastic buckets, a gravel siphon, a small net for catching and moving fish and removing large debris, and perhaps plant tongs and small

pots for planting purposes. A few plant food tablets would also be worthwhile.

SETTING UP THE DISPLAY

Setting up your display can take quite a while, so do this only when you have plenty of time. It is useful to make a sketch of where you plan to feature major decorations such as large rocks and driftwood, because it is easier to move these around on paper rather than in the tank! When this is done, first of all prepare some water in buckets and allow it to stand overnight in the room of the aquarium. This will bring it to room temperature. Test it for chlorine, as well as for its pH, hardness, and other compounds as discussed in an earlier chapter. Make notes of your readings so that you have baseline readings to compare your aquarium water to later on.

Have everything at hand when you commence setting up. Place the tank on its stand and double check that it is very secure. If an undergravel filter is to be used, this must be placed in first. Be sure it's a snug fit; otherwise, water will bypass the main body of the filter and exit via gaps, taking the path of least resistance.

The gravel goes in next. If you wish to create a stepped effect you can use strips of plastic glued to a plastic base to act as retainers for terraces, or you can purchase "walls" from your pet dealer, or use slate or other flat rocks to act as retainers. The ultimate depth of the gravel will range from about one inch in the foreground to 2-3 inches at the sides and rear. By this arrangement, debris and mulm is encouraged to fall toward the front of the tank or terraces, where it is more easily removed.

Before the gravel has reached its full depth, insert the rocks and other decorations. Be sure they are well anchored so that there are no pockets where food could accumulate and decay. Build up around these. The heater and filter tubes can now be placed into position and disguised behind rocks, or placed where they will be hidden by plants.

At this point some water can be poured or siphoned from a bucket into the tank. Let it flow gently onto a saucer, or a piece of cardboard, so as not to disturb the gravel. Now is the time to insert plants, either in small pots or directly into the gravel. The advantage of planting at this time is that the leaves will float on the water and not be in your way, nor will you be trying to plant them in deep water.

With everything in place you can now half-fill the aquarium and assess it. If all is well, finish filling the tank to about one inch below its capacity. Add the hood and power up the filter and heater. (Be sure nothing is plugged into sockets while your hands are in the water!) In order for biological action to commence quickly, you can purchase starter cultures from your pet shop. It takes time for aerobic bacteria to colonize the gravel bed, and thus start the nitrogen cycle. Likewise, plants need time to take root.

During the next week or so you should take regular pH and other readings, as well as see that the heater and filter are operating correctly. Any dying leaves on plants should be removed. Only when all the conditions are satisfactory, and stable(!) should the first guppies be introduced.

Stocking the Aquarium

Initially, you need only two or three guppies, and these should be very healthy individuals. Transport them home as quickly as possible so that the water in their plastic bag does not cool and cause stress. The bag should be floated on the water surface for a few minutes so temperature equalization can take place. Add some tank water to the bag. When you are ready to release the fish, open the neck of the bag and let the guppies gently swim out. The next few days will tell you if the initial inhabitants have settled in and are doing well, in which case you can then start to add more stock—but never stock up too rapidly and risk upsetting the delicate balance that should be taking place. Ideally, after the initial fish have been placed in the aquarium, all further stock should be quarantined as a precaution. This is discussed further in the health chapter.

From here on in it is a matter of making partial water changes, doing routine cleaning and replacement of filter media, and generally keeping the aquarium clean. Of course, observation of your fish is paramount in order that you can quickly spot any that might be acting abnormally.

FEEDING

Compared with the situation that prevailed for aquarists of only about thirty years ago, the present-day hobbyist is absolutely spoiled when it comes to commercially prepared fish foods. There is no longer the need to be trying to rear cultures of live foods that are both messy and rather smelly (although some of the best guppy breeders still do). Vast sums of money have been invested into fish nutrition in order to cater for the needs of the millions of hobbyists worldwide.

FEEDING TYPES

All fish species have evolved to eat certain types of foods, and this is reflected in a number of ways. For example, the guppy has a relatively long digestive tract. This tells us that it eats quite a bit of plant matter, which needs a longer period of digestion than does animal protein in order to be broken down to its basic ingredients. The guppy's upturned mouth indicates it has evolved to be a surface feeder, and that it snatches live foods that alight on the surface. In other words, its diet is a mixture of live foods and plant matter. Such feeding types are called *omnivorous*, as compared to those that are *carnivorous* (predominately flesh eaters) and those which are *herbivorous* (predominately plant eaters). Young guppies are situated more toward the carnivorous end of the omnivore scale. They need to put on body weight quickly, and proteins are the best way of doing

One of Gan's best selling guppies is this redtail guppy which are produced in Singapore at the Gan Aquarium Fish Farm.

this. As they mature they need fewer proteins and more carbohydrates. The latter are the most readily available and easily acquired sources of energy for general day-to-day muscular activity.

From the feeding type, conclusions can be drawn as to feeding habits. Carnivores are able to gorge on a meal, then be relatively inactive while the food is metabolized. Herbivores need to graze steadily in order that there is a flow of food at all times in their digestive tract. The omnivore is somewhere between these two. Translated into feeding regimens, an omnivore is best fed about three times a day: morning, afternoon, and early evening (before the aquarium lights are switched off). If any of the meals must be omitted because of your schedule, the afternoon one would be the best. Young fry do, of course, need more meals per day if maximum growth is to be achieved.

FOOD FORMS

The form in which you provide food to your guppies probably will fall into one of the following categories: flake, tablet, powdered, liquid, freeze-dried, frozen, fresh, and live.

Flake: This is probably the most popular form and is available in a range of ingredient bases, ranging from wholly vegetable to high-protein, and from slow- to fast-sinking to suit the feeding preferences of different species. Extra care must be used when feeding flake foods because they

The red snakeskin guppy produced by Gan Aquarium Fish Farm.

The famous Blond Tuxedo Guppy produced by Gan Aquarium Fish Farm in Singapore.

can easily fall into crevices if uneaten, then decay, to the detriment of water quality. Little and often is the best way to use them.

Tablet: These can either be free-falling, or stuck to the aquarium glass. One advantage of foods placed in set positions is that you can encourage your guppies to feed at given locations. You are then better able to observe their individual feeding habits, and are more likely to notice if any are missing at feeding time—which would prompt you to wonder why.

Powdered: In this form the food is more scattered throughout the aquarium and better suited to very small fry. As with flake food, a little and often is the best method to avoid the risk of polluting the water.

Liquid: These foods are also well suited to very young fry and will find their way, via the water circulation, to those areas of the tank where youngsters may be taking refuge. They are quickly eaten and digested.

Freeze-dried: These are popular and enable high-protein foods (such as tubifex worms) to be fed without the risk of introducing pathogens. They store well and swell as they absorb water.

Frozen: Almost as "hygienic" as freeze-dried, they are the obvious alternative to live foods with respect to the nutritional ingredients they possess. They allow you to feed many foods that ordinarily would either not be readily available to you, or are seasonal.

Fresh: This term is used to

embrace the many foods you can supply from your home kitchen. Examples are fresh vegetables, cheese, and other dairy byproducts, boiled egg, minced lean meats, fruit, cereal, and their byproducts. Of course, these must be presented in a form that can be eaten by guppies. They can be minced, then formed into cubes held together by gelatin, or they can be crushed until very small and offered as is, or they can be passed through a blender and given as a mixed solution. Slivers of meat can be suspended in the aquarium to be nibbled on for short periods, so there are numerous ways these foods can be offered to your guppies. Be cautious, however, as many of these foods will foul the water quickly if uneaten.

Live foods: These include worms (grindal, white, tubifex, earth) of various types and sizes, insects, fish eggs, daphnia, and brine shrimp, to name but a few. Again, some are already very small and so can be fed as they are, but others will needed chopping to an acceptable size. If this does not appeal to you, the answer is to purchase them in the frozen state.

If live foods are caught from natural waters, be aware that they can introduce pathogens into your aquarium, as well as the larvae of insects that may be predatory on guppies.

OVERFEEDING

One of the great dangers for any aquarist, but especially for those new to the hobby, is overfeeding. With guppies and other fishes you simply cannot casually drop a quantity of food into the water on the basis that what is not eaten can be removed sometime later

The so-called Gan Dragon Head Guppy.

PHOTO BY CHEW KENG LOON.

The blue variegated guppy strain produced by the Gan Aquarium Fish Farm in Singapore.

and discarded, as sometimes can be done with mammals, birds, and other land creatures. The situation is made even more problematic because even excessive quantities of food will still appear to us to be a relatively small amount. But that small amount, on a progressive basis and in a small closed system, which is what an aquarium is, can soon have a dramatic effect on the quality of the water. It can result in an increasing pollution rate that the filter system and plants cannot cope with. Your fish (and plants) will become sickly and soon perish.

The remedy is to always watch your fish at feeding time. Place only a very small amount of food in the water and observe how quickly it is all eaten. You can always give a little extra, but you cannot as easily remove the excess. As a guide, the fish should devour most of the food within 2-3 minutes. Small but numerous meals are your best policy initially. In a mature, well-planted tank, your fish will rarely be at risk to starvation. There will always be microorganisms living on the substrate, the plants, and the decorations. Regular siphoning of the substrate, coupled with partial water changes and checks on the pH and nitrite levels, are your means to ensure that pollution is never a problem. Guppies are hardy and extremely easy fish to care for, but this does not mean that a casual approach will suffice.

FEED A BALANCED DIET
Fishes are no different than other animals in that they need a well-balanced diet if they are to

This neon guppy category entry took Third Prize at the Aquarama '93 Guppy Show held in Singapore.

reach optimum size, retain full breeding vigor, and display their colors and fins to best effect. *Balanced* means receiving the required amounts of proteins, carbohydrates, fats, vitamins, and minerals, and in the proper ratios. Achieving balance is not easy because so many factors are involved. Every aquarium is quite unique—even two in the same room are different micro-worlds.

As you gain practical experience you will, by observation, results, and reading, learn more about *balance*. Initially, proceed by ensuring that you supply a wide range of foods in various forms. Do not assume that all commercial foods are complete diets. Read the labels.

By supplying a range of foods you minimize the possibility that some important ingredient is lacking in the diet of your fish. Make feeding an integral part of your husbandry and the results will more than justify the effort.

Winners of the Second Prize in the 1993 Aquarama were these tuxedo guppies.

GUPPY VARIETIES

Guppies may be compared to the most majestic of coldwater fishes—koi—in that while they are seen in a number of recognized varieties, the potential colors and patterns are limitless. New strains continually are being created, and new mutations that may be worthy of selective development appear spontaneously. So, whether you want a particular variety, or just a collection of dazzling-looking fish for your display tank, you have started with the right species.

In this chapter we can only take a brief look at the more obvious fin shapes and color patterns, but these will give you a good idea just what an array of forms there are. It should also be mentioned that, compared to the early years of this hobby, even females can be obtained today in some very pretty color and fin combinations.

When breeding guppies you will find that the mating of two comparable types will not normally produce 100% of the same type and color. This is because very many gene combinations go into producing patterns, colors, and fin shapes. As a consequence, the random way in which genes reassemble themselves at fertilization is such that totally purebreeding varieties are the exception rather than the rule. Dominant genes will, of course, express themselves, but it is the hidden recessives that may come together to create colors,

patterns, and fin shapes that might not have been anticipated based on the appearance of the parents. This is a double-edged sword. It creates enormous problems for the specialty breeder, yet may be greatly appreciated by the average fancier, who looks forward to each brood in anticipation of the array of colors and forms that may be produced.

FINS

There are at least twelve fin shapes to choose from. Some are very obvious, their name making their shapes easily recognizable. Others are not so easily identified and can be mistaken for other shapes. Indeed, the names themselves have changed in some instances, or the same fin shape is known by different names in different areas or countries. These shapes are determined from male guppies; females usually have tails that are rounded, or at least less developed than those of the males.

1) **Deltatail:** A very popular variety, the deltatail exhibits a wide triangular shape that, more than any other, allows the beautiful colors and patterns seen in guppies to be displayed at their very best. Its drawback is that as the guppy ages the thin edges start to break. Also, the tail can be ruined if any of the tank inhabitants are fin nippers.

Red Blond Deltatail developed at the Gan Aquarium Fish Farm.

A blue variegated longfin developed by Gan Aquarium Fish Farm.

The Gan White Diamond longfin guppy.

2) **Longfin:** This is a variation on the deltatail in which some of the fin rays of the tail grow longer.

3) **Fantail:** Another of the broadtail group, this is not as wide as the deltatail, but has more gently curving upper and lower edges.

4) **Veiltail:** This is a wide-tailed variety similar to the deltatail, but not as large.

5) **Ribbontail:** As the name suggests, the upper and lower edges of this shape are more parallel than in the deltatail shapes. Also called the flagtail, bannertail, or scarftail by some hobbyists.

6) **Double Swordtail:** In this popular variety the upper and lower fin lobes are extended like rapiers. If only the upper lobe is extended it is known as a top swordtail, if only the lower lobe it is a bottom swordtail.

The double swordtail guppy developed by Gan.

7) **Spadetail:** Self-explanatory; like the ace of spades.

8) **Roundtail:** This is the basic shape of the wild guppy tail and is basically a spadetail without the point.

9) **Pointed Tail:** This is a

The variegated gold guppy produced at the Gan Aquarium Fish Hatchery.

The Japanese ribbontail produced and photographed by Tanaka.

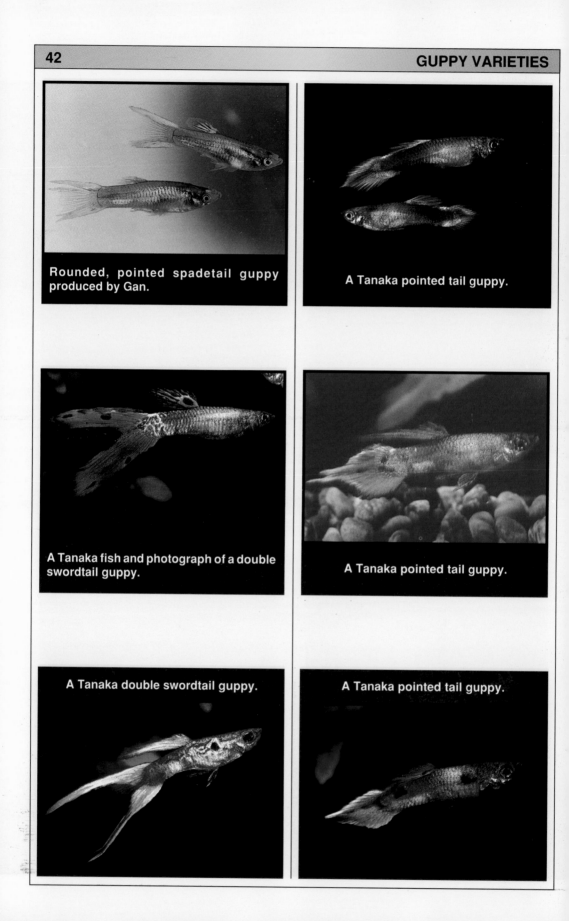

Rounded, pointed spadetail guppy produced by Gan.

A Tanaka pointed tail guppy.

A Tanaka fish and photograph of a double swordtail guppy.

A Tanaka pointed tail guppy.

A Tanaka double swordtail guppy.

A Tanaka pointed tail guppy.

A Tanaka pintail or lacetail.

A Green Diamond Roundtail produced by Gan.

A snakeskin lace produced by Tanaka.

roundtail, but with a central pointed extension to it. Also called a pintail.

12) **Lacetail:** This is rather like the pintail, but the extension is much shorter. Speartail is perhaps a better descriptive term.

PATTERNS

As with the tail fin, only much more so, the number of names applied to color patterns is tremendous. Specialty breeders will apply their own names to particular variations of a pattern they believe to be representative of their stock. However, the following are the basic major genetic variations.

Mosaic: In this pattern, which is one based on the tail fin, though today it can also be seen in the dorsal, there are irregular blotches of color radiating from the caudal peduncle, which is a dark blue color. When the dark blotches are nicely dispersed the effect is quite beautiful, but when they coalesce, or are all toward one side of the tail, the effect is far less striking. There are many variations of the mosaic in numerous color combinations, though the fiery orange-red ground color with black markings is one of the perennial favorites.

Grass: This pattern also was originally restricted to the caudal fin, but also may now be seen in the dorsal. It is a pattern in which the dark markings again radiate from the peduncle, but unlike those of the mosaic, they are fine, and often composed of many small spots in a straight line. The "glass grass" guppy has the spots

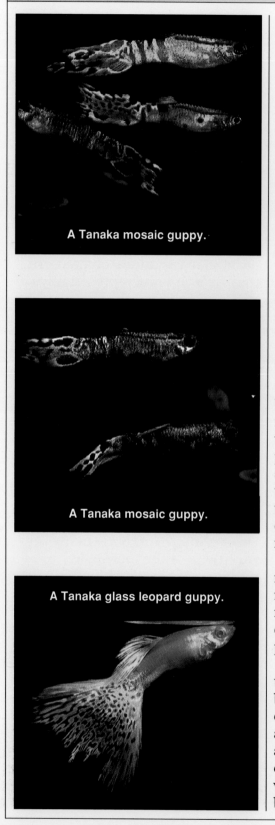

A Tanaka mosaic guppy.

A Tanaka mosaic guppy.

A Tanaka glass leopard guppy.

and fine lines against an almost transparent ground color. The leopard is a very striking pattern in which the markings are reminiscent of those on a leopard. As with mosaics, the grass patterns come in a range of colors, including black, blue, yellow, green, and of course, red. Although the body colors of fish with these patterns can also be very pretty, they look quite plain next to the brilliance of the tail and dorsal fins.

Cobra: Also called the king cobra or snakeskin, this is a body pattern in which there are unbroken lines of pigment that interconnect in a snakeskin pattern. Sometimes the lines break up too much, or they are more striped than snakeskin-like, but even these can still look very impressive. The cobra is available with any of the tail shapes, patterns and colors; thus, a very stunning fish is possible. When these variations are brought together in the same guppy you can image the potential for naming them!

A variation on the cobra pattern is that called the "tiger." As you may deduce, this pattern results in vertical bars of dark pigment on a lighter background that produces a tiger-striped effect.

Tuxedo: As the name suggests, this variety has half the body in black, the other half in any other color. The black may begin just ahead of or behind the dorsal fin, and extends to the end of the caudal peduncle. While a neat vertical line of demarcation between the black and the other

PHOTO BY MP & C PIEDNOIR.

A European snakeskin guppy.

The most popular and productive of Japanese fish breeders is Tanaka. This is the Tanaka Tuxedo.

colors is desirable, this is only seen in the most outstanding of individuals. The variety is also known as the half-black. As with all patterns, the tuxedo is available in a range of colors, and some, such as the blue, are very impressive. It has a blue body followed by the black tuxedo, then blue in the caudal and dorsal fins, with the caudal being edged in black. The flamingo is a red fish with a black tuxedo; again, this is a guppy to behold if it is a good specimen.

The tuxedo pattern is a dominant mutation and can be combined with other patterns on the forebody, as well as with the various fin shapes and patterns.

There are many color combinations that can be seen on guppy bodies, but if you concentrate your attention on the main features discussed in this chapter you will not be at a loss to understand which basic variety you are looking at.

This wonderful guppy is a golden red tuxedo with a long, flowing dorsal with a small slit in the tail.

BREEDING STRATEGY

It would be quite impossible to discuss the genetics of the guppy in a small chapter, so we will review basic breeding strategy and introduce you to simple genetics using examples seen in the guppy.

BREEDING OBJECTIVES

Whenever two animals are mated under domestic conditions, there should be definite objectives that are beyond the simple act of perpetuating the species. It requires no skill to simply have guppies breed, but breeding to produce superior fish with very fixed qualities of color, finnage, and vigor is another matter. This requires great dedication, detailed record-keeping, the ability to make sound judgments based on results, and, it must always be added, a degree of luck in the way the random nature of genes work for you in a program.

The prime objectives of any breeder must always be good health and breeding vigor. You will assuredly be faced with a need to compromise between health and desired characteristics, but never allow this to happen unless you are quite sure there really is no other option. Thereafter, rapidly make health the priority once you have achieved your characteristic objective.

LIMIT YOUR AMBITIONS

As an ambitious breeder, you will want to achieve many things all at once. You may wish to improve the fins and the colors, as well as keep examples of the many varieties. As tempting as this may be, the more numerous your desires, the less likely it will be that success will be achieved in any one area, such as color, fins, vigor, or conformation. Once you understand the basics of genetics, you will appreciate just why this comment is so true, especially when it concerns the large number of offspring that would be involved.

It is always best, even if you keep a number of varieties in a display tank, to concentrate your breeding program on a limited number of objectives. But remember that if you do keep a mixed-variety display tank you must not use the female fish from that tank for breeding; otherwise, there would be little point in specialized breeding. Remember that female guppies are able to store sperm that can be used to fertilize numerous broods of fry. You'll never be able to be sure of the father unless you mate a virgin female with one male. This factor alone makes planned guppy breeding more complicated than it is with most other animals.

ACHIEVING OBJECTIVES

There are two ways in which you can go about improving your guppies. One is by assessing a number of features together, then selecting from those fish that meet your overall standard. The other is to concentrate on one or two features at a time, then concentrate on other features only when the desired result in the former is achieved. Progress is slower in any one feature when you are dealing with a number of features than when you concentrate on one or two. But in the long term, either option achieves your objectives.

When tandem breeding (one feature at a time) is the method used, you must always be careful that, in moving your priorities to the next feature, undue deterioration in the standard of the feature that has already been improved is not a consequence. To limit the possibility of this happening necessitates a "closed" breeding program.

THE CLOSED PROGRAM

The meaning of a closed program is that, having obtained stock of an acceptable standard, you do not continue to use stock from outside sources when its genotype is unknown, and which could therefore hinder the progress of your entire program. Out of necessity, a closed program means you will be inbreeding to some degree. This latter term often is wrongly associated with negatives in the average beginner's mind, so let's apply a definition to it. It is the mating of individuals from the same line: offspring-to-parent, brother-to-sister, etc. In reality, it would be impossible to establish and improve a variety of a species without an inbreeding policy.

There are potential negatives when inbreeding. These can only be overcome by rigorous culling of breeding stock at each generation, but this fact applies to any form of breeding if improvements are to be achieved.

BASIC GENETIC THEORY

You cannot be a serious breeder of guppies unless you understand the basics of how the features you wish to deal with are passed from one generation to the next. You must therefore learn about genetics to at least the level that you can achieve your objectives and avoid pitfalls.

Genes are sequences of DNA that code for a particular trait. Genes are attached to larger structures called *chromosomes*. Some genes act in a major manner in that their presence in a single dose is sufficient to change a feature. Others require two genes to achieve this. Still others work on an additive basis, and the features they control are said to be *polygenic* in transmission. Color and fins are examples of the first two types, size being an example of polygenic action.

Although color and fins are controlled by major gene action, they are also subject to polygenes in the form of those that modify the depth of color or size of fins. These are aptly called *modifier genes*. Another influence over color and fins you will need to be aware of is that of the guppy's sex. Features that are related to the sex of an animal are known as *sex-linked*. These obviously include matters such as physical and physiological differences between the sexes. A few colors and fin types are also subject to sex genes, as compared to most others that are inherited regardless of which sex happens to carry them.

HOW GENES WORK

The chromosomes already mentioned are found in pairs within the body cells. The exception is in the reproductive cells (sex cells). In the guppy (and humans, as well), the chromosomes of the female are designated **XX**, those of the male **XY**.

On the chromosomes, each gene's position is known as its *locus.* On the opposite chromosome of a pair there is a similar locus for that feature. Thus, with respect to a simple color, such as blue, albino, or gold, two genes determine the color, one on each chromosome of a pair at the same locus. When guppies mate, their paired chromosomes separate. Each goes into a sex cell, so that each sex cell contains one of the original chromosomes (thus half the genes) that determined the color and other features of the parent. The sex cells contain one each of all the paired autosomal chromosomes, plus either an X or Y chromosome.

When the sex cells (egg and sperm) unite at fertilization, the paired chromosomes (thus genes) are reestablished. The process is rather more complex than this as far as the genes go, but in essence this is what happens. If the genes of both parents at the same locus are identical or nearly so, the offspring will express that trait in the same manner as both parents. More often, the genes are a little different, and the genetic recombination may create a new expression of a trait in the offspring. Let us look at this more carefully so you will understand.

If a given gene determines that a guppy will have a wild coloration, then if both genes of a pair (one from each parent) are for this expression, it will have wild coloration. If this individual mates with one of a similar type, the only combination of their union will be the wild type. We can show this mating by using letters to represent the genes, which is how you will work out the results of different matings.

There is a major gene that allows all other color genes to express themselves. It is designated as **C**, meaning full color (wild type gene). A wild guppy thus has two **C** genes (one

A grand champion Blond Diamond Roundtail guppy produced by Gan Aquarium Fish Farm.

on each chromosome of a pair). If two similar wild-type guppies mate, the formula will be **CC** x **CC** = **CC.** No other combination of genes is possible.

MUTATIONS

A mutation is said to have taken place when there is a change in the way a gene expresses itself. Something happens that alters the chemical makeup of the gene. It remains at its locus, and creates an

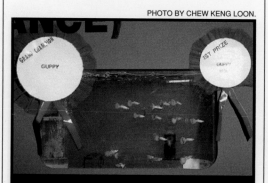

PHOTO BY CHEW KENG LOON.

This tankful of identical guppies won First Prize and Grand Champion in the Neon Guppy Category at the Aquarama '93. Fish produced at the Gan Aquarium Fish Hatchery.

alternative expression to the normal situation (wild type) at that locus. The gene may have variable powers of expression, but three in particular are of interest to us at this level of study.

A *dominant* gene is one that can express itself when present in single dose (just one gene of a pair at a given locus). A *recessive* gene is one that must be present in double dose (both genes of a pair) to be seen in the offspring. When one of each type is present the dominant gene will be seen, but

the recessive is still there. It cannot express itself because it is masked by the more potent dominant. However, it retains its own identity, and can be transmitted just as the dominant can. They both have an equal chance of being passed on to their progeny.

The third type of gene expression is known as *incomplete dominance.* In this, the dominant gene is not able to fully suppress the recessive gene. As a result, the fish may display both gene expressions in the same fish, or an apparent blending between the two types (a light and dark blue, for example). Genes never truly blend, so if they appear to do so it is because of incomplete dominance, or because another pair of genes is affecting them (as is the case with the veiltail variety).

The dominant gene is represented by a capital letter, the recessive by a lowercase letter. The mutational gene is always given the same letter as its dominant alternative. This is so you do not lose sight of the fact that one is the alternative (called an *allelomorph*) of the other. When a pair of genes are for the same expression of a trait, the feature they determine is said to be *homozygous* = purebreeding. When they are for differing expressions the feature is *heterozygous* = non-purebreeding.

CALCULATING EXPECTATIONS

The foregoing provides you with some basic knowledge of genes, so now we can consider how to work out expectations from given pairings. We'll begin with albinism, which is inherited in a simple recessive manner. However, in some fishes, including guppies, albinism is incomplete. By this is meant that it does not suppress all pigments, only the melanins that create black and brown.

In point of fact, many mutations in guppies confound the expectations of genetics, but this does not negate their importance. It is simply that in these and other fishes the mode of transmission is very complex, and still not fully understood for some varieties. But you can be assured that all colors are inherited in a way that follows the rules of inheritance.

A pure wild-colored guppy has the genotype **CC,** while the albino variant is **cc.** If a **CC** fish is paired with a **cc** fish, the wild type can pass only a **C** gene to its offspring, and the albino can only pass on a **c** for its contribution. This is the only potential combination of these two genes, so all the offspring must have the genotype **Cc.** Full color is dominant to albinism, so the first generation all have wild type coloration. They are wild (or normals), heterozygous for albinism. We can now differentiate between two types of normal coloration. The one phenotype (appearance) can result from two quite different genotypes (homozygous **CC** and heterozygous **Cc**). If the heterozygous offspring are inbred to each other we will produce some albinos and some normals. In order to work these out for yourself in other simple recessive mutations, you must calculate every potential combination of the

genes each parent could pass to their fry. In this particular mating of brother to sister the formula would be: **Cc** x **Cc** = **CC, Cc, Cc, cc.** In other words, 25% will be homozygous normal, 50% will be heterozygous normal, and 25% will be albino (homozygous recessive). This means that 75% will look

With many guppies, getting fish to look alike does not mean that they are identical but that they can be recognized as a strain.

normal and 25% will be albino. The only way you can establish which of the wild types are purebreeding (homozygous) is by further matings.

The calculation gives us a theoretical expectation ratio of combinations. These will work out over the long run, though not necessarily a short run (such as one particular brood). This is because they are subject to random selection—much as is the case if you flip a coin. There will be a 50/50 split of heads or tails if you do an infinite number of coin flips, but over the short run some variations are possible. For instance, you could throw three or four heads in a row.

Note that a dominantly controlled feature can be split for a recessive gene, but a recessive feature cannot be split if it is visible in the individual. In other words, a mating of two albinos produces only albinos. Writing the genotype of a split guppy is done thus: Normal/albino—that in front of the slash is visible (dominant), that behind it is masked (recessive). In writing the genotype of the **CC** or **Cc** offspring produced in the sibling mating, this is done as **C-**.

This exceptionally beautiful strain is a Leopard/Tiger with a new kind of tail.

The dash indicates that the second gene is unknown and could be either **C** or **c**. In using the albino as an example of simple gene action involving recessive mutations I must add an important footnote. While the 3:1 ratio is typical of such a mating when breeding two heterozygotes, this assumes that there are no secondary problems that affect the expectations. In the albino guppy there are such complications. The actual results are more likely to be on the order of 53:1 wild to albino. This is because the albino gene in these fish is linked to an inherent weakness, or lethal recessive gene, that results in a very high death rate of albino fry before they are born.

MORE COMPLEX MATINGS

In the foregoing matings we considered only one color locus, that being the one controlling full color. But there are many others. When two loci are involved things are more complex, and even more so when three or more loci are considered. As you increase the number of loci under consideration, so you dramatically increase the number of potential permutations. We will look only at a mating involving two mutations, as this will illustrate what you must do.

Let us pair a blue guppy (genotype **rr**) with an albino, (genotype **cc**). When doing this it is most important that you do not forget to include the full genotype of the individuals, for reasons that will soon become apparent. The blue guppy is actually **CCrr**, while the albino is **ccRR**. Remember, we are now dealing with two loci, that for albino and that for blue. At the albino (full color) locus the blue is normal (non-albino), the albino being normal (non-blue) at the blue locus.

The blue guppy can pass on only a blue gene at the blue locus and a normal gene at the full color locus. It therefore passes the genes **C** and **r** on to its offspring. The albino can pass on only a **c** gene at the full color locus and only an **R** at the blue locus. It thus passes on **c** and **R**. The genotype of the first generation is therefore **CcRr**. Translated into color, all the offspring are normal-looking (wild type), but are heterozygous for both blue and albino.

If these youngsters are inbred

the color ratio expectations are:

9 Normals—1 homozygous (**CCRR**), 2 Normal/blue (**CCRr**), 4 Normal/albino & blue (**CcRr**), 2 Normal/albino (**CcRR**).

3 Blue comprising the following genotypes:

    1 Homozygous (**CCrr**)
    2 Blue/albino (**CcRR**)

3 Albino comprising the following genotypes:

    1 Homozygous (**ccRR**)
    2 Albino/blue (**ccRr**)

1 Albino Blue (Homozygous for both colors) (**ccrr**)

In order to minimize the risk of error in making calculations involving two or more mutations it is wise to use a checkerboard-like arrangement called a Punnett square. The genes that each parent can pass are placed along the horizontal and vertical planes. It is then a simple matter to fill in the blank squares.

SEX LINKAGE

The guppy has 22 pairs of autosomal (body) chromosomes and one pair of sex chromosomes. Most features of the fish are carried on the autosomes, but some, including certain colors and fin types, are carried on the sex chromosomes. With autosomal genes it does matter which sex carries the mutations. This is not the case with sex-linked genes.

This aspect of genetics often confounds the beginner. But it is actually quite simple as long as you always bear in mind which sex chromosome is linked to which feature. If a feature is carried on the **X** chromosome then it can be passed to both daughters and

sons, but if it is on the **Y** chromosome only the males can inherit it. In guppies the mutant dark posterior body and caudal peduncle color is known as *nigrocaudatus* or *tuxedo* (**N**[t]), and is carried on the **X** chromosome, while the iridescent color pattern in this same area is carried on the **Y** chromosome. The mutations are both dominant. If no tuxedo is present, the **X** chromosome will have the genotype of **XN**, which is shown in some texts as **Ch**,

The Rainbow Guppy category winner, First Prize in Aquarama '93.

meaning caudal hyaline or transparent. The use of differing letters for the same locus can cause confusion, so I have used the same letters, as in the rest of this text, for alleles at a locus. The **N** gene is the normal wild type (non-tuxedo) dominant. However, the tuxedo gene is dominant to the wild type. This is indicated by the superscripted "**t**" that indicates it is a mutational gene.

Let us pair a tuxedo female of

XN^t XN^t genotype with a male iridescent which caries no tuxedo mutant, so has a genotype of XN YI^p, where the superscript "p" indicates the mutant iridescent pattern and **"I"** is normal wild type (non-iridescent). Only two permutations are possible from this union.

1) The XN^t tuxedo gene of the female can combine with the non-tuxedo gene of the male to create XN^tXN. This creates tuxedo females heterozygous for non-tuxedo.

2) The XN^t of the female can combine with the YI^p of the male to create XN^tYI^p, which is a tuxedo iridescent male. However, the tuxedo gene is superdominant when combined with the dominant iridescent and results in masking its presence. It is said to be *epistatic* to iridescent. That the I^p gene is present we will now prove. We will mate the male (XN^t YI^p) with a female tuxedo, but which is heterozygous for non-tuxedo. Her genotype is thus XN^tXN. The four potential permutations are:

1) XN^tXN^t = Homozygous tuxedo females;

2) XN^tXN = Tuxedo females split for non tuxedo;

3) XN^tYI^p = Tuxedo masking iridescent males;

4) $XNYI^p$ = Iridescent males.

As the female cannot carry the iridescent gene the males displaying this color (4) must have inherited the gene from their father, even though it was not visible in him due to the presence of the tuxedo gene. Permutation (3) also carries this mutant gene, but is exactly like his father in appearance.

Other genes that are carried on the sex chromosomes include the veiltail, double swordtail (**Y** chromosome) and flavus (yellow-tailed: **X** chromosome). The veiltail is interesting because it results from the interaction of the flavus and double-sword mutant, which are on different sex chromosomes.

From the foregoing you will appreciate that breeding for varieties is a complicated undertaking, for what is discussed here is only the bare bones of guppy genetics. However, it should acquaint you with the most-used terminology. With this knowledge understood, you are now ready to tackle more detailed texts on this subject.

PHOTO AND FISH BY TANAKA.

The huge spots in the tails of these two guppies indicate they are closely related and a genetic variation.

PRACTICAL BREEDING

Although guppies are extremely easy to breed, there are a number of pitfalls that make them very difficult if the object is to be selective with regard to colors and fin shapes. Furthermore, you also must provide safety for the newborn fry; otherwise, their mother, and any other fishes near them (as in a community tank), will take delight in consuming them as a tasty snack.

The major problem confronting the breeder who wishes to breed for certain colors and fin shapes is that the female can store sperm from a given mating and use these to fertilize up to four or more additional broods. This fact alone can play havoc with the serious breeder's program, and is the main reason why there are so many "mongrel" guppies to be seen. If the sexes are not separated at the earliest possible time, the likelihood is that the young males will mate with their mother, their sisters, and any other willing females in the aquarium! With this fact in mind we must first consider the basic breeding life of the two sexes.

PHOTOS AND FISH BY TANAKA.

What beauty in these guppies; not only are they similarly colored but their tails are almost as long as their bodies.

GUPPY BREEDING LIFE CYCLE

The guppy has an average lifespan of 12 months, somewhat less in strains that have resulted from a program in which breeding vigor has been sacrificed at the expense of purely esthetic qualities (color pattern, fin size and shape). Clearly, in such a short time, and given the sperm-storing capacity of the female, much, perhaps all of her breeding life could easily be wasted if she should be mated by an undesirable male. You must wait until she has used up all the sperm packets before she can then be mated to the desired male. Unfortunately, you cannot tell when this has happened, and most breeders consider such a female lost to further breeding.

The breeding life cycle can be broadly divided into the following time frames:

Birth to 4 weeks: This is the period in which the gonopodium develops in the male. Once this is complete he can mate. This is the time when the sexes must be separated.

5-9 weeks: During this period the colors really start to show themselves and the fins are getting larger. The sexes must have been separated by the early part of this period if virgin females are to be obtained.

10-26 weeks: This is the time when the guppy is at its most beautiful, and when maximum breeding capacity is reached. Shortly after the start of this period the female suddenly increases her size compared to the male.

27 weeks onward: Now very mature, the colors and breeding capacity start to recede, the more so if water conditions are not ideal.

free-swimming youngster is about 28 days. It can be shorter or much longer depending on the strain, the individual parents, and the environmental conditions, food, and especially the water temperature. As the female gets near to the time of spawning her abdomen will swell. You will see the typical dark or gravid spot at the rear of the abdomen that indicates fetal development. The heads of the fry may be seen through the abdominal wall in the gravid spot shortly before they are actually born.

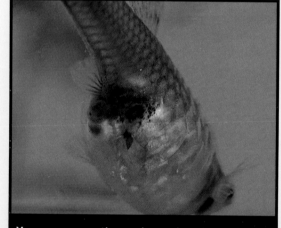

PHOTO BY DR. HERBERT R. AXELROD.

You can see the unborn fry through the translucent belly of the female guppy.

THE BREEDING TANK

You will need a number of small breeding tanks of 10-gallon capacity. The female will need to be kept in one of these, while at least two more will be required to house the youngsters once they are old enough to be separated into single-sex groups. The more guppies you breed in terms of numbers or strains, the more tanks you will need. This is why it is wise to specialize in just one variety, and also to commence with a small program and let it expand slowly according to your interest and available cash. It is

BROOD SIZE

The first brood is normally of about 10 fry. Subsequent broods increase in number within the range of 20-100, though 25-40 is perhaps typical. The factors that influence brood size are the strain of guppy, its breeding vigor, and the conditions under which it has been kept with regard to temperature and water quality.

INCUBATION

The time it takes the fertilized egg to develop and be born as a very easy for the beginner to become overwhelmed by an over-ambitious program.

The tank should be freshly prepared for each breeding. It should be well-planted and contain a heater and a simple sponge or box filter. Mating will take place quickly because the male guppy normally has strong procreative desires. After a few days the male can be removed so he does not cause stress to the female by habitually chasing her around the tank.

BREEDING TRAPS

You will need a breeding trap in the tank in order to provide safety for the newly born fry. A number of models are made commercially. The trap is essentially a small cage in which the female is housed as she nears term. Its sides have small openings large enough for the fry to swim through, but too small for the female. If it is large enough to house a few strands of floating plants, so much the better, as this will help relax the female. Do not place her in the trap too early, as she may become overstressed and abort her brood. A few days before she is due to give birth you can

raise the temperature by 2-3ºF: this will encourage her to have her babies.

REARING THE FRY

Young fry need to be able to feed on a continuous basis, and making this so in the first days of their lives is particularly vital. The nauplii of brine shrimp (*Artemia salina*) are an excellent food; brine shrimp eggs and the directions for hatching them can be obtained from your pet shop. Prepared fry foods also are available in liquid, powder, or micro-flake forms. If the fry are underfed the larger, more aggressive youngsters will soon devour the more timid individuals

This strain of boldly marked guppies has disappeared from the domestic scene. If they reappear, be sure to get some as they produce very highly colored guppies. Photo by Tanaka who developed these fish.

because the latter will not have received their share of the food. If you have utilized a good-sized breeding tank it is now that it will pay dividends, especially if it is well-planted. The more space the fish have, the better they will grow. A large rearing tank also avoids the need to relocate the fry until they are ready to be sex-grouped. Moving any fish from one environment to another is always stressful, all the more so for youngsters.

QUALITY CULLING

It is very important that from the time they are born until they are mature you remove any individuals that display deformities of any kind—those with incorrect physical conformation, poor fins, and an inability to swim correctly. As the fish mature you will be selecting for quality of fin and color pattern, so that ultimately you will retain only a very few fish for onward breeding. Most breeders opt to use the culls as feeder fish for larger, predatory fishes such as cichlids.

Clearly, once the young virgin females have been separated from the males you cannot place them into a community of guppies or other fishes. They should be given their own tank until they are ready to be bred at about four months of age. Once their breeding life is over they can be placed in the community tank, because their smaller litters will be unlikely to survive in this location.

From the foregoing you will appreciate that serious breeding of guppies is not as easy as you may have at first thought. You are always confronted with the problem of keeping females from casual matings. If you stay with one variety, then at least in the event unwanted matings take place you will still have a recognizable variety from such matings.

An old strain of bronze guppies was utilized to prepare this un-named Japanese strain produced and photographed by Tanaka.

MAINTAINING GOOD HEALTH

Guppies are very hardy little fish, but their small size does mean that if they contract a problem they can very rapidly deteriorate and die. When a fish does develop a condition or disease the added problem is that all other fish sharing the same water will of course be exposed to it. The cliché that prevention is nine-tenths of a cure is very true where fishes, especially guppies, are concerned.

Once one or more fish have become ill you are confronted with another dilemma. Should the fish be treated *in situ*, or be removed to a hospital tank? If they are treated in their aquarium there is the real risk that the medications may destroy the beneficial bacteria of the filter system, and this will increase your problems. Furthermore, many pathogens, once established in a closed body of water, may be capable of surviving the treatment in their spore stage. No sooner have you apparently overcome the

Aquarium hobbyists are able to take advantage of the many remedies and preventatives that have been formulated specifically for use with guppies and other tropical fishes. Photo courtesy of Aquarium Products.

problem than it reappears! The potential list of conditions and diseases in fishes is huge. With this fact in mind, this chapter is devoted mainly to prevention techniques and what to do in the event a problem is found. You should then refer to more detailed texts in order to try and pinpoint the cause of the problem.

Pet shops carry an extensive range of health products, and your dealer is the person to talk to if you suspect, or have, a problem. Most of the likely conditions you might encounter can be treated if these are dealt with promptly.

WATER CONDITIONS

Just about every disease and condition in aquaria are the result of a breakdown in care. Here is a list of *some* of the ways pathogens get into your aquarium and how to reduce the risk of their entering your water:

1) During the initial setting up of the aquarium you did not clean

every addition to it. Pathogens could thus have been present even before a fish was placed in the tank. Plants must be cleansed using an appropriate treatment from your pet shop. Rocks, gravel, and all decorations should be rinsed with very hot water before use.

2) The water should be "mature" and at the correct temperature before a single fish is added. If the nitrogen cycle has not been completed this will greatly stress the initial fish and raise the probability of a problem. Remember, a number of pathogens are ever present, no matter what you do. Do not stress the fish and give them an opportunity to attack!

3) The initial fish are best quarantined before being placed into a display tank. It is far easier to strip down a quarantine tank if problems are encountered than to do the same with a newly established system, complete with all of its decorations and extra water volume.

4) The initial and all additional fish should be obtained from a very reputable source, otherwise you will simply transfer their problems to your tanks.

5) Never risk overstocking the aquarium, as this can result in stressed fish. Such individuals are far more susceptible to illness than contented fish.

6) Ensure that routine cleaning is maintained on a regular basis and that all tools used are sterilized (hot water and/or a rinse in strong salt water) before and after each use.

THE QUARANTINE/HOSPITAL TANK

This is without doubt your best safeguard from transferring problems from the seller's tanks to your own, regardless of how good the seller's reputation is—even they can have problems. The tank can be small (5-10 gal) and should be sparsely decorated using artificial plants and small ceramic flowerpots to provide refuge. It will need a heater and a simple box filter, together with moderate to dim lighting. Make sure the water is the same temperature as that from which the fish are coming. During the quarantine period this can then be adjusted to that of your main aquarium if there is a difference.

The isolation period should be about 14-21 days. Add about one half a teaspoon of salt to each gallon of water, and this will prove beneficial in eradicating low levels of many bacteria. During the isolation period observe the fish carefully for signs of problems (to be discussed shortly).

In the event you are treating sick fish, add the medicine to the water as per the manufacturer's instructions only, assuming you have a positive diagnosis of the problem. Once the isolation/treatment period is over, adjust conditions back to those of your display tank and then reintroduce the fish to the main tank. Then strip the treatment tank and thoroughly clean it. Repeat this operation immediately before its next use.

IDENTIFYING PROBLEMS

There are two types of diseases in fishes. There are those that display some outward sign of their presence, and those that do not. Your attention will be focused on the former. If a number of fish start to die without displaying external signs, your first thoughts should be to the water quality and the possibility that there is a toxin. First, you should discuss the matter with a fish expert, preferably one who can examine the fish and your aquarium. A water specimen should be analyzed by a chemist if possible. At the very

pronounced, which may be too late. 1) Lack of appetite. In a large community of guppies it is easy to miss the fish that is not consuming its normal amount of food. 2) Erratic movements: This heading includes sudden darting across the tank for no reason, rubbing against hard objects, or swimming in a lopsided manner. The problem is probably parasitic or related to the swim bladder. 3) Breathing problems: The fish will gasp at the surface for air, and its gills will be

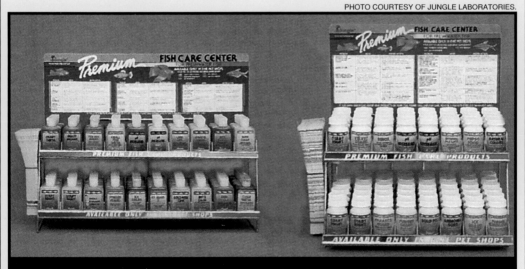

Many different remedies, preventives and tonics are available at pet shops.

least, you should conduct the water tests (nitrite, pH, etc., discussed earlier) for a content list. Normally, however, fish will display some indication of problems and the following are some items to look for.

Behavioral oddities: Only by observing your fish on a daily basis will you become acquainted with each fish and its habits. Without this knowledge the chances are that you will only perceive a behavioral change when it is very

reddened and open. The problem may be parasitic, bacterial, or the result of excess ammonia or nitrites in the water, assuming aeration is adequate. 4) Listlessness: The fish seeks a refuge behind plants or decorations. It may rest on these, or the substrate, showing little interest in what else is happening in the tank. As it may be hidden from view, a head count of your fish will show up any that are missing.

Physical Signs: Any abnormal signs are unhealthy in your fish. These include swellings, abrasions, loss of color (dullness caused by excess mucus resulting from skin infection), missing bits of fins (these may result from nipping by other fish or from disease), spots, cotton-like growths, and visible parasites attached to the skin.

WHAT YOU SHOULD DO

The golden rule when applied to any potential illness is *Never do nothing.* If you decide to wait and see how things are tomorrow you may awake to see one or two fish, or an entire collection, floating on the surface or laying on the substrate, dead. You must note all of the physical and behavioral signs, as well as the water conditions (temperature, pH, nitrite, and so on). Relate these to your dealer and act on the advice given.

Clearly, you must decide on the severity of the problem. Is just one fish ill, or are many showing problems? If just one, then it should be removed immediately and placed in a hospital tank. If a number, much will depend on the illness or disease. Generally, if many fish are ill you might as well treat them in the main tank; raise the temperature a few degrees and effect the remedial treatment. However, if this route is

A Purple Glass Variegated Guppy produced by Gan Aquarium Fish Farm in Singapore.

taken it is suggested that once things are normal again the tank is stripped down and set up again. This is obviously time-consuming, but it may avoid a repeat of the problem. Transferring all of the fish to a hospital tank may not be practical (due to the size of tank needed) and could stress the fish, which is not recommended when they are already stressed by illness.

If fish are treated in the main tank, try to obtain medicines that will not kill the beneficial bacteria. Do not turn off the filter system at this time, because this will reverse the nitrogen cycle and prove counter-productive, though this could happen anyway if the medicines kill the beneficial bacteria. Even so, you still need the aeration and water circulation facility of your filter system. If the tank is heavily stocked it would be prudent to decrease the numbers as soon as possible in order to both reduce the risk of the spread of disease, and to reduce the pressure on the filter and aeration systems.

Take out only those fish that seem very healthy. This action just might save a number of the fish from actually contracting what might prove to be a fatal disease that wipes out those that remain in the original tank.

GLOSSARY OF USEFUL TERMINOLOGY

Albino: A pure white animal that displays no pigment whatsoever. It is red-eyed. In guppies albinism is only partial, and restricted to the melanin pigments; thus, other colors such as yellows and reds can be seen.

Chromosome: The structure that carries genes.

Dominant: A gene that expresses itself visually when in single dose.

Epistatic: Said of a gene that is able to mask the presence of one or more other genes. Albinism is a typical example.

Filtration: A collective term applied to any process, be this mechanical, chemical, or biological, that removes unwanted substances (solids or gases) from a given volume of water.

Gamete: A male or female reproductive cell; a sperm or ovum (egg).

Gene: The basic unit of heredity.

Genotype: The total genetic composition of an individual, combining both visual and "masked" genes.

Hardness: An expression to indicate the amount of salts in a given volume of water. It can be measured in various ways, and may be temporary or permanent.

Heterozygous: An individual having unlike genes at a given locus, thus producing unlike gametes for the characteristic in question. Non-purebreeding.

Homozygous: An individual having like genes at a given locus, thus producing similar gametes for the characteristic in question.

PHOTO BY TANAKA.

Tanaka produced many mutants which were never sold internationally and thus have no name.

Purebreeding.

Locus (plural, Loci): The fixed position on a chromosome at which a gene, or one of its alternative forms (alleles), is located.

Mutation: A sudden change in the way a gene expresses itself. It creates an alternative characteristic (allelomorph) at the locus or loci of the gene(s) involved.

Oviparous: Egglaying. The embryos are nourished by the egg yolk and hatch outside of the female's body.

Ovoviviparous: Producing eggs that hatch in the oviduct of the female, but are not directly, or only partially, nourished by her. Livebearing.

Ovum: An egg; the sex cell of the female.

pH: A logarithmic scale that is used to indicate the acidity or alkalinity of water based on the number of hydrogen and hydroxide ions present. pH 1.0-6.9 is acidic, pH 7.0 is neutral, and pH 7.1-14.0 is alkaline.

Phenotype: The visual appearance of an individual. Two fish may have the same phenotype, but may not breed alike. Their

recessive's presence.

Sex-linkage: The state that exists when the heredity of a gene is located on a sex chromosome is linked to the sex that carries it. Genes located on the X chromosome can be passed to either sex, those on the Y chromosome can be inherited only by the males.

Species: A group of animals that will interbreed in the wild and are reproductively isolated from all

A champion double swordtail guppy developed and photographed by Tanaka

visual similarity may derive from different genotypes.

Poecilia reticulata: The current scientific name for the guppy.

Polygenic: Said of a characteristic that is inherited on a quantitative basis involving many genes, for example, size.

Recessive: A gene that must be present on both chromosomes of a pair in order to be visually apparent. The exception is a gene carried on the sex chromosome—a sex-linked gene, where no locus exists on the other sex chromosome of a pair, so there can be no dominant gene to mask the

other groups. The lowest obligatory rank in a formal classification.

Sperm: The sex cell of the male.

Viviparous: Producing eggs that are retained within the uterus of the female where they are nourished by her. Livebearing.

Wild type or Normal: Terms used in genetics to indicate the natural phenotype of a species as compared with any mutational forms.

Zygote: An ovum that has been penetrated by a sperm, resulting in a fertilized egg that contains all of the genetic material for the new individual.

INTRODUCTION

Although a number of fishes have gained notoriety in films, books, and television, two are blessed with especially unsavory reputations. These are the great white shark of "Jaws" fame and the piranhas of South America. You can't keep a shark in your aquarium, but the piranha you can. As with all animals that have gained infamous reputations, the reality is often somewhat less than the legend. This said, the notoriety of these fishes is no figment of the imagination. They are extremely dangerous and quite capable of doing exactly what they are famed for doing.

A school of piranhas can reduce a wounded crocodile to its skeleton in the time it would take to haul it out of the water on a length of rope! It would take even less time to devour a human being. However, these fishes are not swimming around South American waters seeking out humans and other mammals for dinner. If they were, no animal would ever venture into piranha infested waters. In this sense, therefore, they are rather misunderstood.

"Piranha" does not refer to a single species, as is often thought by the average person, but is a common name applied to a group of species, all of which are very closely related. Some are more dangerous than others. They are relatives of many of the most popular and peaceful fishes (tetras and the like) that are seen in the aquarium hobby, as you will learn in the following chapter.

Piranhas cannot be regarded as species to be recommended to the first time aquarist. Their diet and water requirements must be well suited to their needs. They will, once adult, require a large aquarium. Being carnivorous (and potentially savage) they cannot be kept with other fishes without the risk that they may either nip pieces from them or devour them. Indeed, they can only be reliably accommodated in the average home situation with their own kind and, even then, while they are juveniles. Even in this situation there will be the risk that some of them will be mutilated or eaten by their slightly larger or stronger tank mates.

They are, therefore, a collection of species supported in the aquarium hobby by a number of enthusiastic specialists. Often, they may be seen in a pet or aquarium store because their fame makes them an instant source of curiosity, thus an "attraction" for the stores that have them on display.

In the following chapters all of the information that you will need to know about piranhas from a hobbyist's point of view is detailed. If you then feel you would like to own a piranha you are advised to seek the advice of an enthusiast, or a store manager that is experienced with them, before venturing any further.

You will not, of course, ever be housing a collection of them in a single aquarium (this would have to be an enormous tank), but even so you are cautioned that even a single fish can inflict a severe injury to a hand or finger carelessly placed into the water. These are not the sort of fishes you should obtain on a passing "whim," no more than you would obtain a poisonous snake, or spider, just to say you owned one. Given due respect for the potential of what their dental work can do and proper care to their needs, piranhas are an interesting group of fishes that will always command attention and have a nucleus of serious devotees.

PHOTO BY DR. KARL KNACK.

Juvenile *Serrasalmus nattereri*. These are probably the most popular piranhas and most prevalent in the Amazon River system.

WHAT ARE PIRANHAS?

There are about 20,000 species of fishes living in the various waters of our planet. There are more fishes than all the other vertebrate animals (mammals, birds, reptiles, and amphibians) put together. As all life evolved in the water, and most of our planet's surface is covered by water, this is perhaps not surprising. It is most probable that there are still a few thousand fishes yet to be discovered.

A fish may be broadly defined as an animal that lives in water, breathes via gills throughout its life, moves by means of fins, has a body supported by a backbone, has a covering of scales (some have secondarily lost them), and whose body temperature is controlled by the environment (poikilothermic, meaning variable, but commonly known as cold-blooded) rather than internally (homoiothermic, meaning the same temperature, or warm-blooded). Using this definition, whales, dolphins, and their like are not fishes (they are mammals), nor are many of the other creatures you can find living in water that sport the name (ex. starfishes, cuttlefishes).

Over 90% of all fishes are bony, as compared with the sharks, rays, skates, and the like in which bone is replaced by cartilage. There are also a number of jawless fishes. The bony fishes are all placed in a group (class) called Osteichthyes. This is divided into many groups (orders) in which the member species have a number of common features that warrant their being grouped together. One of these orders is the Characiformes. Within this order are many famous aquarium fishes, such as the anostomins and leporinins (family Anostomidae), the hatchetfishes (family Gasteropelecidae), the pencilfishes (family Lebiasinidae), the distichodontins (family Distichodontidae), and the very extensive list of tetras, the many species that carry the name characin, and those that are the subject of this book, the piranhas (family Characidae). Although the name characin is generally reserved for the family Characidae, it has also been used extensively for species that are allocated to other families of this order. The infamous piranhas have sometimes also been housed in their own family, Serrasalmidae, but most recently are considered as being included in the subfamily Serrasalminae within the family Characidae. In the subfamily Serrasalminae are included two major groups, the basic plant eaters (*Colossoma, Metynnis,* etc.), which total about seven genera with about 60 species, and the piranhas (also known as the caribs) proper, with four genera (*Serrasalmus, Pygocentrus, Pygopristis,* and *Pristobrycon*) and about 50 or so species, many of which are still to be

PHOTO BY GLEN SCOTT AXELROD.

Dried piranhas with beads for eyes are a typical souvenir sold in the Amazon. The fish are caught, soaked in formalin, rinsed and then dried. They are mounted on Amazonian hardwoods, painted, varnished and sold to tourists.

described. Many of these piranhas are not dangerous, but it is the few that are that give them all their evil reputation. The classification of these fishes is discussed in more detail in the chapter on the individual species.

DISTRIBUTION & HABITAT

Characins and their allies (of which there are over 1,300 species) are found mainly in Central and South America, with only about 200 species native to African waters. In evolutionary terms, they are thought to have existed as a group for maybe up to 150 million years in the case of the earliest types, with the division into African and American forms occurring about 90 million years ago. The piranhas are found only in northern South America (the Amazon, Orinoco, Paraguay, and San Francisco river systems as well as in the rivers of the Guianas), but most are indigenous to the great Amazon basin. They live in many rivers and their tributaries, as well as within lakes.

Piranhas are possibly at their most dangerous to humans when living in tributaries and waters that become cut off from the main river during dry periods. When this happens, and they have devoured most of the available fishes that form the greater part of their natural diet, they will of course attack anything that will satiate their at times ravenous appetites. However, like many fishes, piranhas can endure quite long periods without feeding, and many of them survive these periods of drought to return to the main river following heavy

PHOTO BY DR. HERBERT R. AXELROD.

This huge *Serrasalmus notatus* was caught in the Brazilian village of the Caiapo Indians in October, 1964. The fish was 19 inches (about 50 cm) long. It is doubtful that the village or the large piranhas exist any more.

seasonal storms.

Only when mammals (which include humans) are wounded do the more ferocious species smell the blood and attack. Most of the gory stories you hear about them are straight from the imagination of novelists and script writers but, this said, they clearly remain potentially among the most savage and dangerous of all freshwater fish species.

There is no doubt that a number of people have been killed by these fishes—but this is a fact that can be said of hundreds of animal

species. Indeed, there are dozens of animals that kill more people every year than piranhas have accomplished over many decades, yet these fishes have been elevated to a status that has no relationship to its real threat to humans.

Basic Anatomy

The piranha is a typical fish with comparable anatomy, but it does have certain features not always seen in all fishes. Of course they do have the dentistry that is related to their mode of feeding. I cannot discuss anatomy in any detail, so what follows is a basic overview.

Shape & Size: Depending on the species, piranhas are discus to rhomboid

Serrasalmus striolatus.

in which a dip or indentation can be seen above the eyes. The jaw muscles of the dangerous species are also larger and more powerful.

Color: Piranhas cannot be regarded as very colorful fishes. The range is from silver through blue-green to brown, with many sporting spots or bars on their sides, others having some red on the body and in the fins. Refer to the species chapter for more details. The fact that some species show great variation in color as they mature has made their identification very difficult. This has resulted in many names being applied to what are actually different ontogenetic forms of the same species.

Fins: There are two basic types of fins in fishes, the median (unpaired) fins and the paired fins. The piranha has a larger dorsal fin followed by a small adipose fin. The anal fin and the caudal fin

Serrasalmus elongatus collected in the Lago Las Pupunhas on the Rio Madeira. It was 12 inches (30 cm) long.

in shape, being strongly laterally compressed. A few species, such as *Serrasalmus elongatus*, are atypical in that, as the name suggests, they have a more elongate shape. Size again depends on the species involved, the larger examples reaching 40cm (22in), with 22-31cm (8.5-12in) being a typical length for most species once they are adult. This fact should be taken under advisement very carefully before these fishes are considered for the home aquarium.

In broad terms there is a shape distinction between those species that are held to be very dangerous and those that are less so. The dangerous species have a more rounded head profile compared to the less dangerous species

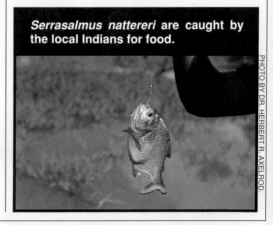
Serrasalmus nattereri are caught by the local Indians for food.

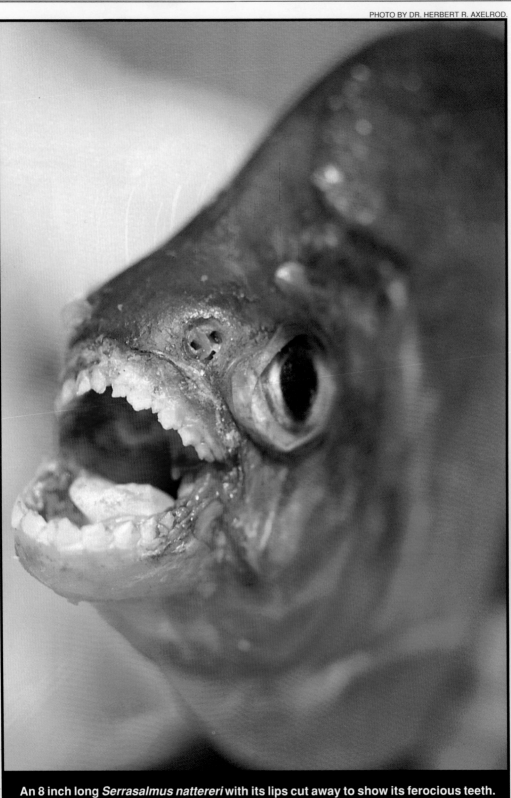

An 8 inch long *Serrasalmus nattereri* with its lips cut away to show its ferocious teeth.

Many of the Amazonian explorers catch and eat piranhas. They are usually gutted and fried in a pan. They are very plentiful and easy to catch with hook and line and a piece of raw meat as bait.

having evolved to rip pieces of flesh away from their victims. The teeth of each jaw, when closed, work rather like old animal traps. They interlock with each other to form a serrated cutting edge.

Scales: The scales of the piranha are of two types. The majority of scales covering the body are cycloid. This means they are of a basically round shape with smooth outer edges. You see only part of the scale, most being buried in the dermal layer of the skin. The second type are modified scales found along the ventral edge of the fish called scutes. In structure, the scales of a piranha are typical of all bony fishes. They are translucent, not colored as many non-aquarists and beginners may think, and they are loosely held in the skin, thus easily shed.

Digestive Tract: As is the case with all predatory animals, the intestines of the piranha are short when compared to that of

A 12 inch black piranha, *Serrasalmus niger* with its lips cut away to show its dangerous cutting teeth. This species is very dangerous.

complete the unpaired fins. The caudal fin is variably indented to almost forked, as befits fishes capable of rapid movement in spite of their non–streamlined body.

The paired fins include the pectorals, which are situated just behind the lower part of the gill aperture on either side of the body, and the ventral fins. The ventral fins are found on the ventral sides, almost about the middle of the fish, and, because of their location, are also called abdominal fins.

Mouth: The mouth is bounded by fleshy lips. Its opening in piranhas is terminal to slightly superior, with the lower jaw protruding beyond the upper. This indicates that piranhas normally attack from below. The teeth may be in various arrangements, but are carried on the dentary bone below and the premaxilla above. They are relatively uniform in shape, and very sharp,

PHOTO BY AQUA PRESS, MP & C. PIEDNOIR.

A mature specimen of *Serrasalmus nattereri* awaits unsuspecting prey as it hides behind a piece of wood.

herbivorous feeders, and the stomach is larger. This is because protein (flesh) is digested more readily than plant matter, whose hard cellulose walls require a longer time in the intestines.

Circulation: The circulatory system of the piranha is typical for that of most fishes. It is a simple single circulation. The heart is not four chambered as in mammals, but two chambered. Blood is pumped from the ventricle into the ventral aorta, thence to the gills via capillaries that go into each gill arch so that the blood can be oxygenated. It

adequate rather than good. In the murky waters of a river distance vision is hardly of use to a fish. It largely lacks binocular vision, but its field is good, with the eyes being placed laterally. The eyes can rotate very well so it is able to see anything approaching it from the front, sides, and rear.

More important to the piranha is its sense of smell, and its ability to detect any disturbances in the water. It is able to decipher the latter with remarkable ability, so it can sense a fish or animal that is floundering. Along the sides of its body are

PHOTO BY DR. HERBERT R. AXELROD.

Serrasalmus spilopleura.

is then picked up by more capillaries which feed the dorsal aorta, which transports it to the rest of the body.

Other capillaries gather the deoxygenated blood and transport it into the venous system (veins) which carry it back to the atrium of the heart. It passes via a valve into the ventricle to commence the circulation again. The heart is situated on the ventral part of the body just below and behind the gill arches, the safest position for it to be in.

Senses: The eyesight of a piranha is

a series of small openings that connect, via sensory cells, to the brain. This is called the lateral line, which also connects to the inner ear (fishes have no middle or outer ear).

The slightest vibrations in the water are picked up and amplified in the inner ear. In all cyprinids there is a special mechanism to assist in detecting changes in the water pressure surrounding the fish. This is a series of bones that connect the swim bladder to the inner ear and it is called the Weberian apparatus. Via these various mechanisms a piranha is very aware of all

that is happening in its murky watery world.

It is because of a fish's great sensitivity to vibrations transmitted in water that the annoying habit of people tapping on the glass of fish tanks offends aquarists, who appreciate that this action can be distressing to these sensitive creatures.

Reproduction: Fishes reproduce in one of three ways. Some lay eggs that hatch outside of the body (oviparous), others lay eggs that hatch inside the female (ovoviviparous), while others have offspring that our nourished by the female and are true livebearers (viviparous). Piranhas belong to the first group, being oviparous (egglayers). More details are given in the breeding chapter.

Social Status: Piranhas are mostly schooling fishes, the size of a school varying depending on the type of species and environmental conditions. They roam along stretches of rivers and tributaries as opportunistic feeders taking whatever comes their way. During feeding frenzies it is quite normal for them to bite each other, but only when times are really hard will they actually become cannibalistic. Within the confines of a small aquarium they may attack each other, not so much because they are hungry (assuming they are well fed), but due to the pressures of stress brought about by the limited space they have.

However, although basically social, these fishes are just as capable of being solitary predators—much like a wolf is a pack animal, but is also a highly efficient predator when on its own. As a solitary hunter it will hover in reeds or near rocks and rely on stealth to catch its prey. Some species will actually swim within schools of their prey, suddenly taking one of these (or a piece of them) while the school is unaware what has happened. Piranhas will also prey on other piranhas, some being specialized to nip fins or scales of larger species. There is a tendency to regard the piranha as being a more important predator within its ecosystem than it actually is.

A school of *Serrasalmus nattereri* are safe from each other's attack because they are well fed. If they were to be left unfed, they would attack and eat each other.

PHOTO BY AQUA PRESS, MP AND C. PIEDNOIR

AQUARIA, FILTERS, LIGHTS, AND HEAT

The first thing that you must understand if you have any thoughts of keeping piranhas is that you will need a large aquarium. This becomes even more important if you contemplate keeping two or more in a single tank. It is, of course, possible to keep a number of very(!) young individuals together in a moderate sized unit, but as they grow (and they can grow very fast) you would soon be faced with either having to house them in a larger tank, or having to obtain more tanks.

However, even overlooking the question of the tank size with respect to its life supporting ability, just as important is the fact that even young piranhas may start taking pieces out of each other. It is best to view these fishes as single tank occupants until a great deal of experience is gained with them. Other fish species (such as catfishes) may then be added. These might be able to cohabit with piranhas, but there is always the proviso that unless the aquarium is very large it is more than an even bet that sooner or later some problems will arise.

Individual specimens are often seen in quite modest sized aquaria, but this is not really the way to keep these fishes unless it is for short duration, such as at an exhibition. These are comparatively large fishes and need a home that allows them some capability of moving around. You should think in terms of an aquarium that has a capacity of at least 23 US gallons. The larger species will need tanks three to five times this size!

Not only will these aquaria take up quite a large amount of space in the average room, they will also be exceedingly heavy— more than enough to crash through any but the strongest floors. The average pet or aquarium store is unlikely to stock tanks suited to the larger species, so it will normally mean placing a special order. These are not species suited to the financially faint hearted when it comes to setting up the aquarium and obtaining examples!

AQUARIUM SHAPE & CONSTRUCTION

The best shape for an aquarium is the tried and tested rectangle. It displays the fishes best and is the most practical shape from a maintenance standpoint. It will also be a less expensive option.

With respect to its construction, you should ensure that it is constructed of the very finest materials. Large tanks hold a lot of water, which exerts considerable pressure on the glass panels. Any weaknesses may put you at risk of having the tank suddenly burst. The water will be all over the floor and will ruin your carpets—and this will not endear you to your neighbors if you live above them in an apartment. With these possibilities in mind it would be wise for the owners of a large unit to check whether or not they are well covered with insurance.

CALCULATING NEEDED TANK SIZE

Aquaria are sold either by their length or by their volume, the latter being the usual method in the US. You will need to know the volume in order to establish its weight when full of water, for calculating dosages of any medicines to be added to it, and for working out the size of the filter system needed to achieve the correct turnover of water. The surface area is important inasmuch as it determines the amount of oxygen that can be absorbed by the water, almost regardless of its volume.

This in turn influences the number of fishes that can be kept in that volume in the absence of auxiliary equipment. However, no doubt you will be using the latter, and the fact that you will probably only be keeping one or two piranhas means that it is unlikely you will risk overtaxing the oxygen retaining capabilities of the tank.

CONTENTS

© c.

Distributed in the UNITED F.H. Publications, Inc., One T.F.H. Plaza, Neptune ne UNITED STATES to the Bookstore and Library Tr ic. 4 20 Boston Way, Lanham MD 20706; in CANADA lies c., 27 Kingston Crescent, Kitchener, Ontario N2B Sartelon St. Laurent-Montreal Quebec H4R 1E8; in CANADA to nwell Publishing Ltd., 1 Northrup Crescent, St. Catharines, Ontario L2M 6P5, D by T.F.H. Publications, PO Box 15, Waterlooville PO7 6BQ; in AUSTRALIA AND THE SOUTH PAC C by T.F.H. (Australia), Pty. Ltd., Box 149, Brookvale 2100 N.S.W., Australia; in NE EALAND by Brooklands Aquarium Ltd. 5 McGiven Drive, New Plymouth, RD1 New nd; in Japan by T.F.H. Publications, Japan—Jiro Tsuda, 10-12-3 Ohjidai, Sakura, 285, Japan; in SOUTH AFRICA by Lopis (Pty) Ltd., P.O. Box 39127, Booysens, 2 ohannesburg, South Africa. Published by T.F.H. Publications, Inc.

MANUFACTURED IN THE
UNITED STATES OF AMERICA
BY T.F.H. PUBLICATIONS, INC.

PIRANHAS

KEEPING & BREEDING
THEM IN CAPTIVITY

PROF. MANOLITO PINKGUNI

Nonetheless you should be aware of the accepted formulae for stocking rates in tropical(!) aquaria: Allow 75cm² (12in²) of surface area for every 2.5cm (1in) of fish, excluding its tail. Using this formula we can take a sample tank, one with a length of 93cm (36in) and a width of 45cm (18in), and work out the size of a piranha it could house.

Surface area = L (93cm) x W (45cm) = 4,185cm²

Divide by 75cm² = 55.8 units of surface area

Multiply units by 2.54 = 142cm (56in) of fish body.

A more rapid way to work out stocking levels is to divide the surface area by 30. Thus, in the sample given 4,185 divided by 30 = 139.5, which is close enough. In reverse, you can establish the total length of the adult fish body and multiply this by 30 to give the minimum surface area needed. The example tank, without additional aeration, would thus adequately suit any single piranha, and 2-5 of most species, without extra aeration, such as that provided via the filtration system. However, a 93cm long tank would give a 25cm piranha only a modest amount of room to swim in.

Even allowing for the extra oxygen needs of a large fish, such as the piranha, which has much body bulk, it can be seen that while surface area calculations may well be excellent for working out stocking levels of small tropical fishes, it is not quite as useful for a large species kept alone. With these fishes you must take into account the sheer size of the fish, so that it will have adequate space in which to move around.

AQUARIUM VOLUME

Apart from the other aspects of volume already discussed, of major importance is that it provides the total environment in which your piranha will be living. By the time the aquarium is furnished with a substrate, rocks, plants, and possibly filter equipment, the available swimming area remaining can be surprisingly small—depending on how much aquascaping has been done. As a general recommendation, you are always wise to obtain a unit that is somewhat larger than the one you had originally planned to get.

You can never have too much space in an aquarium, but you can certainly find that there is too little. It is also easier in many ways to maintain a larger unit than a smaller one. Water temperature, and its quality, tend to remain more stable the greater the volume concerned (which is why seas and oceans have less fluctuation in their temperatures than do rivers and lakes).

To calculate the volume of a tank, multiply its length times its width times its depth. Having established the volume you can easily work out the weight. You need not worry about the weight of the rocks and equipment because, from a practical standpoint, this will roughly approximate the weight of the water they displace.

Further, you will not be filling the tank to its capacity. Even allowing for the hood and its lights, the potential weight of the

PHOTO BY DR. HERBERT R. AXELROD.

The Berlin (Germany) Aquarium has a huge aquarium in which a large school of piranhas is exhibited. They are not dangerous when they are well fed.

water by volume will be a sound guide for consideration of the support strength you are likely to need to prevent it from going through the floor.

USEFUL CONVERSIONS AND CALCULATIONS

Volume = Length x width x depth. Example: 93x38x38cm = 134,292 cu. cm.

To convert volume to gallons: There are 3,785 cu. cm in a US gallon (or 231 cu. in. in a US Gallon). There are 4,537 cu. cm in a British gallon (or 277 cu. in. in a British gallon).

Example: 134,292 divided by 3,785 = 35.5 US gallons, divided by 4,537 = 29.6 UK gallons, and divided by 1,000 = 134 liters.

To convert US gallons to British (Imperial) gallons divide by 1.2, to convert British gallons to US gallons multiply by 1.2.

1 US gallon = 3.8 liters
1 British gallon = 4.55 liters
1 US gallon weighs 8.3 lb.
1 British gallon weighs 10 lb.

1 Liter weighs 2.2 lb
1 Kilogram = 2.2 lb.
1 US gallon = 3.8 Kilos
1 British gallon = 4.55 Kilos

From these various equivalents you can see that a 35.5 US gallon tank would weigh 295 lbs. This is equal to that of a very overweight person, though it might not look it. Such a tank would hardly be considered large by piranha standards. Given the weight factor you should consider where the aquarium is to be placed in your room, taking into account the numerous factors detailed in the following chapter.

AERATION & FILTRATION

The objective of aeration is to ensure that the water contains adequate amounts of dissolved oxygen for the fishes to breathe (via their gills). Filtration is to ensure that the water remains in a clean, unpolluted state. Although these two processes are separate entities, they can be combined in the filtration system. It is therefore not necessary to have a separate aeration system

Serrasalmus denticulatus is not one of the dangerous piranhas, but every piranha can bite, so keep your hands out of their aquarium!

PHOTO BY ANDRE ROTH.

It is an absolute necessity that piranha aquariums be filtered and aerated. Your pet shop can show you filters suitable for the capacity of your aquarium. Photo courtesy of Penn Plax.

unless you wish to create esthetic effects from rising columns of bubbles.

You should, however, understand the principle of aeration. Air is passed from a small pump down a tube and exits via a special porous material, such as stone, to which it is attached. The rising column of bubbles burst at the surface. In so doing they disturb this and create mini waves. These effectively increase the surface area, thus that which is exposed to the atmosphere. This enables more oxygen to enter the water than would be the case if the interface was still. The rising bubbles on their way to the surface to release their air have little effect on the oxygen content of the tank. The size of the bubbles is regulated via the air stream from the pump, by valves or clamps on the piping, by the air stone size, or by a combination of these. Aeration has the secondary benefit of creating water circulation, by drawing water up behind the bubbles, thus helping to avoid temperature stratification in the deeper tanks.

FILTRATION

The filter system that you utilize in your aquarium is the main means by which you extract unwanted materials, gases, chemical compounds, etc., in solution or suspension from the water. The secondary method of their removal is via partial water changes. This keeps them in a diluted state, thus taking some of the work load from the filter system.

Filtration is achieved via one of three processes, which often act in more than one capacity.

1. Mechanical: This is effected by passing the water over or through any material that will prevent onward movement of solids. For example, if water is passed through synthetic filter wool, gravel, ceramic rings, glass chips, and their like, solid detritus will be trapped. Periodically the container holding the mechanical filter is removed and cleaned. The finer the filter, the more readily it will become "full" and slow down

the rate of water flowing through it. In a very large aquarium the mechanical filter may be of a two stage type—coarse and fine. This filter will also act in a biological capacity.

2. Chemical: This filter works on the basis that it attracts chemicals that are either in a dissolved state or are in very fine suspension so that they are able to pass through the average mechanical filter medium. The addition of other chemicals to the water (ion exchange resins) in order that these can combine with unwanted compounds to create a safe compound, also falls under the heading of chemical filtration. They are technically not filters but are grouped with them for practical reasons.

Charcoal is the most often used chemical filter as it adsorbs compounds and gases, thus rendering them harmless. Other examples are zeolite, and the various resins just mentioned. However, if chemical filters are not cleaned on a regular basis they may reverse their action and discharge the compounds back into the water. They thus become ineffective. Further, if medicines are added to the aquarium these filters must be removed otherwise they will remove, or negate the benefit of, the medicines.

3. Biological: This is actually a chemical process because it involves the conversion of ammonia to nitrites, then to nitrates, as discussed in the previous chapter. It is called biological filtration because living organisms are utilized. For these to survive they require a richly oxygenated surface on which to live. This can be the gravel substrate, rocks, and even the equipment. This form of filtration also acts as a mechanical filter. It is very important that biological filters are kept clean so that their oxygen supply remains high.

In the case of gravel cleaning is best accomplished by skimming the gravel with a tube siphon or gravel cleaner. If the gravel is removed during a major cleaning it should be washed in clean, cool to warm, water (never hot) with no chemicals added. These

may kill the beneficial bacteria. Likewise, when medicines are used check to see whether they are harmful or non destructive to the biological filter bacteria.

Filtration systems are available in many forms, from simple foam cartridges, through canister filters, to highly complex external units that may utilize ultraviolet light for killing microorganisms and protein skimmers for removing excess organic matter. The filter system may be internal, undergravel, or external. It may even be in a separate filter tank, and it may contain a heater for warming the water as well.

The latest external filters have bio-wheels to increase the biological action. These are said to be superior to the undergravel filters, which are loved or hated, depending on the experiences of various aquarists.

All of these filters work on the same principles. They draw water from the lower parts of the aquarium, where it will be the dirtiest and the least oxygenated. This water is then passed through one or more types of filter media before being returned to the surface of the tank via a tube or a spray bar. This return water agitates the water surface, thus increasing its oxygen content and allowing carbon dioxide and other gases to escape.

With respect to the needed flow rate of the filter, this will of course be dependent on numerous factors, such as the size of the tank and the number of fishes, thus the speed with which the tank water is being polluted. However, as a general guide you will need to pass the water through the filters about 3-4 times per hour. When purchasing your filter system check with your dealer that this will be achieved for the volume of water your aquarium holds.

The most popular filters at this time for your needs will be the external canister, power, or bio-wheel filters (which are also external). These have excellent turnover capacities and allow you to service them more easily than in-tank models, which also take up valuable space in the aquarium.

Undergravel filters are extremely efficient if they are set up correctly—much

less so if they are not. As you want to minimize the number of times you may have to place your hands in the aquarium, it is perhaps better to use external filters.

LIGHTING NEEDS

Although you have a wide choice of lamp types, these ranging from tungsten bulbs through various forms of spotlights to fluorescent tubes, it is the last named that you should commence with. They cost less to run, are cool running, and are available in a spectral range suited to meet specific needs. Modern aquarium hoods are designed to accommodate these, some having built in reflectors as well.

Choose the spectral range of the lighting with care. Those that are excellent for encouraging plant growth will have a shorter life-span than will regular daylight tubes. They will also alter the natural colors of the fishes and the aquarium contents—but they will promote healthy plants. This may be a major consideration to you — remember that green algae is also a plant!

Regular daylight tubes will give a more natural lighting, but they are far less effective in creating esthetic appeal, or highlighting the colors of the fishes. If the illumination is too bright, this will encourage heavy algal growth and can make the unit look too "stark." A nice balance can be achieved by featuring one daylight tube and one of those that are biased toward the blue or red end of the spectrum.

The lights (lamps) you select for your piranha aquarium are very important for the well-being of your fish. Your pet shop can help you select the proper lamps. Photo courtesy of Penn Plax.

Unlike the situation with tungsten and spotlights, tube lighting wattage is related to the length of the tube. As this increases so does the wattage. There are different opinions as to how to calculate the amount of light (wattage) needed for an aquarium, so the following will be only general recommendations.

Fluorescent: 10 watts per 31cm (12in) of tank length, or 10 watts per 900cm^2 of surface area.

Lighting must take into account two aspects. One is subjective in that each aquarist's idea of what they perceive to be attractive will differ. The other is objective in that it must meet the needs of the plants if they are to flourish. These two realities allow for quite a range of experimentation in order to arrive at a satisfactory compromise. Bear in mind that the apparent life of a fluorescent tube will greatly exceed its effective life. This is because its beneficial rays will diminish over time and lose their value to the plants even though the tube is still emitting satisfactory viewing light. It is therefore wise to routinely replace tubes about every 6-9 months, depending on how many hours they are being used over a 24-hour period.

Piranhas live in regions that have approximately equal periods of night and day. However, you may find that this may be excessive and result in too much algal or other rampant plant growth, or the reverse, depending on the wattage's of lights being used. You must adjust this either way until, once again, a satisfactory balance has been achieved. Also, ensure that the water surface and cover glass are kept free of dust and dirt, and that the tubes are kept clean.

If not, much of the light's benefit will be lost to the aquarium.

In a very deep tank, fluorescent lighting will not penetrate to the lower depths sufficiently enough to provide good plant growth. Spotlighting may be needed. However, when these are used you must be sure that there are sufficient shaded places where the fishes can avoid the intense brightness of these lights. If you wish to feature the more exotic plants, these are best added only after you have gained greater knowledge on the use of lighting, because this may be critical to their survival—as will the water conditions they need.

You should bear in mind that piranhas tend to prefer somewhat subdued lighting, as would be found in rivers over which there is a generous forest canopy, or shaded parts of the river.

HEATING

As with lighting, there are various ways in which a volume of water can be heated. We will restrict ourselves to combination heater/thermostats as these are by far the most popular. Be sure to purchase one of the well known name brands recommended by your pet or aquarium store. Do not obtain any from sources, such as supermarkets, or other places where there is no staff that can give you good advice on the brands they stock.

The best heater/thermostats will have a pilot light to indicate when the heater is working, and will have been preset so you can select the desired temperature before placing the heater in the water. Quality heaters operate at a very high degree of efficiency, and have a good life span. Even so, it is always wise to have a spare heater on hand just in case the one in the aquarium should malfunction.

In a large aquarium it is prudent to use two heaters, neither of which is capable, by itself, of taking the temperature beyond the desired level. At the same time, if one should fail the other should be able maintain the water at a safe temperature until the faulty one is replaced. If only one powerful heater is used it could raise the temperature to a dangerous, even lethal, level should the thermostat stick in the "on" position.

Deciding what the wattage of the heater(s) should be is subject to very diverse recommendations in aquarium circles. This is because there are many variables that must be taken into consideration. If the heater is very powerful it will be switching on and off continually, and heating the water at a rapid rate when "on". If it is under powered, it will be working for excessive periods, thus reducing its effective life. It may also be incapable of maintaining the needed heat if the ambient temperature of the room falls below its normal level. The larger tanks will maintain their heat for a longer period of time than will the smaller units. The critical factor with heaters is their ability to raise the temperature from that of the room to that needed in the aquarium.

Taking all of these factors into consideration, and assuming the room temperature will never fall 10ºC below that required in the aquarium, you can work on the basis of 4 watts per gallon. If the room temperature might fall more than 10º, you should use 5, 6, or more watts per gallon, depending on just how cold the room gets. In actuality, if a room is subject to this sort of temperature drop overnight it would be very wise to place some insulation, such as cork, on the outer sides and rear aquarium panels to help conserve heat.

A 50-gallon tank will need 200 watts at 4 watts per gal. This can be provided via two 100 watt heaters spaced so as to give even heat distribution throughout the tank. This is more efficient than if a single 200 watt unit were used.

Even though the heater has a thermostat, do not rely completely on this. Always have at least one other accurate thermometer placed on or in the aquarium. Your pet shop has a selection ranging from external stick ons, through internal suction and free floating types—there are even microchip models.

It is very important that the temperature remains as constant as possible. Fishes react very badly to sudden changes of more than a couple of degrees within any 24-hour period. This is especially so if the temperature drops. This is another reason to obtain quality heaters, the quality comment applying equally as much to filter systems and most other aspects of the aquarium hobby.

Serrasalmus nattereri in this beautiful portrait looks almost harmless. Don't be fooled! These are dangerous fish both in Brazil and in your aquarium.

UNDERSTANDING WATER PROPERTIES

The fact that the average non–aquarist has little understanding of water properties is evident from the number of fishes that die each year as a direct result of this ignorance. Probably the best example of a lack of knowledge is seen in goldfish housed in globes that are totally inadequate as an environment in which to keep a fish. As a result, many perish before the owner seeks advice and obtains more suitable accommodations.

A piranha is far more demanding of its water properties than a goldfish, so you must understand their basic needs before even thinking of obtaining one of these — or any other fish species for that matter. Although it may seem that there is a lot to learn, it is not really difficult if you take each aspect one step at a time. Once you have set up your aquarium you will find that it is merely a matter of making routine checks to ensure that all is well. In the following text no assumption is made about your previous knowledge about aquarium keeping. Nothing of importance will be overlooked.

THE THREE WATER TYPES

Water can be divided into three broad types from an aquatic standpoint. These are salt (marine), estuarine, and fresh. Most fish species live in either pure fresh water or pure salt water, with only a relatively few being capable of living in or moving between these two major water types. Piranhas are strictly freshwater fishes. Their body fluids are more concentrated than that of the water they live in, the reverse being true of marine fishes. Through a process called osmosis, freshwater fishes are continually taking in water via their skin and gills and losing salt. To avoid the problem of over–hydration they drink little water and excrete a very dilute urine (between 5 and 12% of their body weight). Marine fishes do the reverse to avoid dehydration.

WATER TEMPERATURE

The temperature of a body of water has a considerable influence over its properties. It controls the amount of oxygen (and other gases as well) it can contain (the warmer it is the less oxygen it can hold). It influences the feeding habits of fishes—as the temperature of the water rises the appetite increases, until a point is reached beyond which they then decrease their food intake again. It influences breeding ability, growth, and resistance to diseases.

As a result of these many influences, fish species have evolved mechanisms to be able to live in water that displays a given range of temperatures. If they are placed in waters that have temperatures that are outside of their normal range they will quickly succumb to illness. Some fishes, for example goldfish and guppies, are very adaptable to temperature variables, as well as to other water properties, as long as these changes are very gradual. They are thus described as being very hardy fishes. Other fishes are less forgiving if their owner does not provide the needed conditions. Piranhas are among these fishes. The temperature range for most tropical species is 70-85°F (21-29.5°C), with 77°F (25°C) being an optimum level for piranhas.

ACIDITY & ALKALINITY (PH)

Water can range from very acid to very alkaline depending on where it comes from. If it is flowing over rather soft, easily dissolved, rocks it will tend to be alkaline due to the amount of salts the rocks contain. If it is flowing over hard insoluble rocks it will be neutral. If the substrate is composed of a great deal of organic matter the water will be acidic.

In order to determine the value of this property of water, aquarists use what is known as the pH scale. This is a measure of the number of hydrogen and hydroxide ions

in the water. The scale runs from 1-14 with the mid point, 7, being called neutral—it has equal numbers of these ions. When there are more hydrogen ions in the water it becomes more acidic. When more hydroxide ions are available the water is more alkaline. A difference of one unit equates to a ten fold change in the acid or alkaline content of the water.

The piranha is native to waters that are rich in organic matter, so they are acidic. The pH range for most fishes is 5.5-7.5, with 6.6-6.7 being the optimum for most species. You can test water for its pH value using any of many kits available from your pet or aquarium store. Every kit comes with clear, easy to follow instructions. In the popular types you add a particular number of drops of a reagent to a sample of the aquarium water and compare the resulting color change with a chart that indicates the pH. You can obtain more accurate electronic indicators, but these are rather expensive.

The pH of water is affected both by the temperature and by other chemicals in the water. It will display a natural variation over any 24 hour period, so tests are best done at the same time of day on a regular schedule. The pH of water will affect the amount of oxygen the hemoglobin of the blood can take up, as will the amount of carbon dioxide, so you will appreciate that living in water is very complex and requires that at least the basic properties—such as pH—are kept as stable as possible.

WATER HARDNESS

As you are probably aware, water can range from very hard to very soft—in the former it is hard to obtain lather from soap, in the latter very easy. Likewise, you will be aware that if the water is hard, kettles and pipes "fur" and will soon become blocked. As with pH, fishes have evolved to live in waters of a given hardness or softness. If the values are not correct for the particular fish, the delicate membranes of the gills are effected, as are the body cells. The result is obviously an inability to breath correctly, as well as other maladies.

As a guide, piranhas prefer water that is just slightly hard. There are various ways in which hardness can be expressed, the most popular being German degrees (dGH) and parts per million (ppm). The former measures the amount of calcium oxide in the water, the latter its calcium carbonate content. You can convert one to the other in the following manner (the less used Clark's (English) measurement is included for completeness):

One Clark degree = 14.3 ppm

One American degree = 17.1 ppm

One German degree = 17.9 ppm

Using ppm as the measurement, the following hardness states are generally defined:

Monitoring the water in which your piranhas are maintained is very important. Your local pet shop will be able to supply you with various water test kits to measure pH, hardness and many other characteristics. Photo courtesy of Wardley Products.

0-100 ppm	= Soft
100-200 ppm	= Slightly to Moderately Hard
200-300 ppm	= Hard
300+ ppm	= Very Hard

The dGH recommendation for piranhas is 10, which is equal to 179 ppm. You need not worry if the hardness is not quite that suggested because fishes can tolerate a small

variation as long as you maintain this as a steady constant once your fishes are established. This comment applies to many aspects of water properties. It is when these parameters fluctuate rapidly that problems will usually commence.

There are various test kits available from your pet or aquarium dealer by which hardness can be measured. Changing the hardness of your water is discussed in chapter 4.

CHLORINE

If you are using city water, you should be aware that it will have been treated with numerous chemicals in order to make it safe for you to drink. The concentrations of these chemicals varies from one locality to another—and from one period of time to another. Although these additives will not harm you they can, depending on what they are, be very dangerous to your fishes. Chlorine and chloramines are two prime examples of chemicals that are added to city water supplies that have adverse effects on your fishes. These can damage their delicate gill membranes and cause breathing difficulties.

Chlorine is easily removed by letting the water stand, whereupon the chlorine dissipates into the atmosphere. You can speed the process up by vigorously stirring (aerating) the water periodically, or by adding conditioning tablets obtained from your pet dealer, this latter being the most convenient way. Chloramines will require chemical conditioner treatment because they are far more stable than chlorine.

THE NITROGEN CYCLE

Another very important aspect of aquarium keeping is related to the process known as the nitrogen cycle. In this process, various waste products, such as fecal matter, decaying uneaten food, dead microscopic organisms, and the dead leaves of plants, all break down to form ammonia or ammonium. These are lethal to fishes even in very small amounts. By the action of bacteria they are converted to nitrites, which are no less toxic. In turn, the nitrites are converted into nitrates which are far less toxic, and which are utilized by plants as a source of food. The nitrobacter bacteria that convert nitrites to nitrates require a plentiful supply of oxygen and for that reason are called aerobic bacteria. These various bacteria are present in the atmosphere, but it takes them a long time to colonize the substrate and other surfaces in water. If fishes are introduced into an aquarium that does not have a large enough colony of these bacteria, the result will be that dangerous nitrites will be present. The fishes will be unable to breath adequately and may be

One of the best and most welcome aquarium accessories is the Automatic Water Changer which allows you to change the water, in full or partially, without carrying heavy buckets of water. Every pet shop has this invaluable tool. Photo courtesy of Aquarium Products.

PHOTO BY DR. HERBERT R. AXELROD.

A *Serrasalmus eigenmanni* as a juvenile.

seen gasping at the surface as though the water lacked oxygen, which may not be the case. This situation is known as the "new tank" syndrome and is easily avoided if you apply correct techniques and are patient when setting up the aquarium. You can purchase bacterial starter cultures to speed up the nitrogen cycle, or you can dangle small slithers of meat in the water which will also help the process get started.

Aquarists may also transfer some substrate gravel from a mature tank to a new one so that the bacteria on the gravel help to establish a new colony. However, unless you are absolutely sure that the gravel is coming from a very healthy tank, this route is best avoided. There is always the risk that the gravel may contain the spores of pathogens (disease causing organisms) or the eggs of parasites. You can purchase test kits for ammonia, nitrites, and nitrates. But, due to the interrelationships of these compounds, you can assume that if the nitrite reading is zero, or very close to this, the other conversions are being effected satisfactorily. When an aquarium is first set

Living plants can flourish in a piranha aquarium if they are provided with the proper nutrient base to get them started. Photo courtesy of Aquarium Products.

up the nitrite levels will fluctuate widely, so you must wait until you are getting constant low readings before introducing any fishes. Even then, only one or two small individuals should be added, so that the bacterial colonies can build up in proportion to the amounts of potential pollution that the fishes, food, and so on, create. Ammonia will not be a problem if the water is even slightly acidic, which it will be for these fishes—it will be ammonium that is the danger. The reverse is true if the water is alkaline.

The whole process of the nitrogen cycle is made more efficient if you install a sound filtration system. This will greatly increase the aeration of the aquarium, and in particular that of the substrate.

METALS AND GASES

All metals, such as iron, copper, and zinc, can be dangerous at certain levels—especially copper. With this in mind it is always prudent to allow a faucet to run for a few seconds. This gets rid of the water that may have been standing in metal pipes. Likewise, avoid using rocks that may have traces of iron or other contaminants in them.

Carbon dioxide is a gas that is essential for healthy plant growth. It readily dissolves in water to form carbonic acid. Fishes release this gas via their gills as a byproduct of respiration. If excess carbon dioxide is present this will lower the amount of oxygen the blood cells can accommodate. Aquarists may introduce this gas into tanks in order to promote healthy plant growth, but should be aware of its danger to fish respiration when the level reaches 35 mg/l. Under normal aquarium conditions, the carbon dioxide level should not be something that will concern you. It is mentioned so that you are aware that fish respiration is complex and influenced by many factors due to the permeable structure of the gill membranes and the cells of the oral cavity.

UNKNOWN AND TRACE WATER PROPERTIES

In the same way that scientists do not know every single constituent of foods, every component of tainted water is not known, "tainted" water meaning water that is not absolutely pure and free of any additional compounds. The aquarist cannot know what compounds are in the water being used, or how they will combine or cause dissociation of other compounds.

A closed body of water, such as an aquarium, can suffer a build-up in the quantities of these unknown or trace chemicals to the point that they have a deleterious effect on the fishes. To avoid this possibility it is always recommended that you make regular partial water changes. This will at least ensure that these unknown "agents" are kept in a diluted state. About 20-25% of the water can be replaced every 2-3 weeks.

DETRITUS

The amount of dead or dying plants, together with the mulm and other detritus in suspension, are obvious indicators of how dirty an aquarium is. A dirty aquarium should be avoided at all costs because it is the precursor of all manner of problems. By the use of gravel cleaners, siphon tubes, and the regular cleaning of mechanical filters, you will greatly aid the efficient biological processes that are taking place. At the same time you will be denying most pathogens the sort of conditions they prefer in order to build up their numbers.

From the foregoing it is hoped that you will have gained a greater insight into the properties of water. You should now be aware that you cannot simply turn the faucet on, fill an aquarium, heat it, and then release fishes into it—not if you expect them to survive more than a few days at best. To a fish, water quality is as important to it as clean fresh air is to you. Indeed, a fish in the comparatively microscopic confines of even a large tank is less able to adapt to poor water conditions than you are to poor air. The water quality of your aquarium is the most important thing you need to understand in order to ensure that your piranha will live a contented and healthy life.

PHOTO BY ANDRE ROTH.

This beautiful *Serrasalmus gibbus* is rarely seen in the aquarium. It thrives under aquarium conditions.

FEEDING PIRANHAS

The piranhas have gained an evil reputation for being very greedy meat-eaters. However, there are more herbivorous piranha species than there are those with carnivorous diets. But even the herbivores are not beyond taking small fishes that will fit easily into their mouths. This is as true of goldfish and koi as it is of the more infamous piranhas. We will be looking at the carnivorous diet for it is the piranhas of this type that this book is essentially about.

In the wild, piranhas are both predators and scavengers—much like the hyena is in Africa. They are more than capable of killing any animal that lives in, or enters, their domain. However, their basic diet comprises small fish species, and those of any size that are sickly or wounded. They will also eat invertebrates, indeed, anything that comes their way when they are hungry.

What should be remembered with regard to any flesh-eating animal is that it does eat vegetation, but not in the direct sense. When it kills its prey the entire carcass is eaten. Within the intestinal tract of its prey will be vegetable matter in various degrees of breakdown. The predator thus consumes this partially digested vegetation and obtains valuable vitamins from it. These are added to those it obtains from meat and those that it is able to synthesize in its own body. The piranha also gains important minerals from the bones of its prey, so it has a completely balanced diet. When not feeding live prey to captive specimens, it is important that this need for a balanced diet is given major consideration.

OPTIONS FOR FEEDING PIRANHAS

You can feed your piranha in one of three ways. You can give it live foods, dead foods, or a mixture of both. Most aquarists do not like the idea of feeding one fish species to another, though a number of them use such a regimen. Fortunately, your piranha can survive very well on a diet that is no longer in the land of the living—if you prefer this method.

These fishes will hunt any smaller fish species placed into their aquarium. They will also consume those that are dead. They will eat worms of most kinds, as well as other invertebrates. Pieces of meat, poultry, and fish will be greedily taken, as will proprietary fish foods that are frozen, dried, flaked, or cubed, if these have a high protein base. Finally, you can make up mashes of various items, which can include eggs, meat, cheese and their like, and combine these with a pasty porridge to bind them together. The piranha will consume all.

In other words, these fishes can be fed much as any of the other smaller carnivorous fish species for aquaria, it being a case that the quantity will have to be much larger, and will therefore be more costly. However, taste is an acquired sense. You should not assume every piranha is a ravenous glutton that will eat just anything at all times. When their appetite is satiated, or nearly so, they will show disinterest in some foods, and bite only at favored items

If the notion of feeding live foods does not seem aberrant, you can purchase the unwanted surplus fishes produced by many aquarists, such as those who breed goldfish and guppies. Pet shops also sell these "feeder" fishes. Dead day-old chicks and small mice can also be fed to piranhas.

HOW MUCH TO FEED AND WHEN

Young piranhas need more meals per day than adults. This is especially so with fry, otherwise they will start devouring each other on the basis of the weakest gets eaten first. We will discuss the feeding of fry in the chapter on breeding. Juveniles and adults should be fed enough to satisfy their appetites. This is determined on a trial and error basis for each individual fish.

What you must try and avoid is polluting the water with more food than the piranha will consume at a single feeding. This means that you should feed small amounts at a time. Watch to be sure that all the food is being taken. When the piranha shows disinterest in further morsels, this is the time to stop. Note the amount you have given and repeat this at the next feeding. Over a couple of weeks you will establish fairly accurately what each piranha needs to satisfy its appetite, and thus remain in a healthy condition.

This is the pattern of their feeding habits in the wild. They may in fact go for days without food, then will gorge themselves as the opportunity presents itself. Some owners will imitate this pattern in their aquaria, feeding the piranhas only two or three times a week—but in larger quantities of course. If you prefer to feed them daily this is just fine.

The most important aspect is that the fish is receiving enough nourishment to maintain its health, and that the regimen is on a regular basis. The potential risk when

PHOTO BY DR. HERBERT R. AXELROD IN BARCELOS, BRAZIL ON THE RIO NEGRO.

This turtle was slaughtered and left at the edge of the river to bleed. It was attacked immediately by a school of piranhas which devastated the turtle in less than one minute!

With regard to the number of feedings, this is subject to varying views. An adult can manage quite well on a single meal given at a regular hour most convenient to you. A juvenile will be better off having two feedings per day. Carnivores are able to consume larger quantities at a time than can herbivorous species. They are then content to rest while that food is being digested.

fishes are not fed daily is that you may forget a meal, so they get very hungry. This would be a disastrous state of affairs if you have two piranhas living together. The possibility would be that one of them might start to view the other as its next meal!

It is important that you always observe your fishes when they eat. By so doing you will be well acquainted with the habits of each piranha. When a fish is ailing the first,

and sometimes only, indication of this will be in its feeding habits. If you can pick up on any decrease or disinterest in its food you will of course keep a closer eye on the fish, and start to explore the reasons for this loss of appetite. You will be looking for further behavioral changes that would confirm that the fish has a problem.

FOOD SIZE AND SUPPLEMENTS

Although piranhas will snap at quite small foods, their size clearly suggests that they should be fed appropriate sized foods. Pieces of meat or dead fish should be large enough to allow them to utilize their razor sharp teeth to bite into them, rather than simply swallowing them whole because they were hardly worth biting!

When raw chunks of meat are fed, it must be remembered that these are deficient in certain needed dietary constituents. It is therefore wise to impregnate the meat with a suitable vitamin supplement. However, if you are feeding a varied diet that represents a good balanced diet, then additional supplements should not be needed. Indeed, your piranha can suffer from the negative effects of too many vitamins as much as it can suffer from a lack of them.

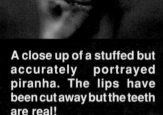

PHOTO BY DR. HERBERT R. AXELROD.

A close up of a stuffed but accurately portrayed piranha. The lips have been cut away but the teeth are real!

INFLUENCES ON APPETITE

Appetite is subject to various influences that you should be aware of. Possibly the most important of these is the water temperature. As the temperature rises toward the upper limit for the species, their appetite increases. Once past this limit, however, it will decrease. Conversely, as the temperature falls below that preferred by the species it will decrease, and eventually cease altogether—as will the fish if the temperature is that low!

The age of your fish will also influence its feeding needs. A healthy growing piranha will consume more than a mature adult. It must put on a lot of muscle, as well as have adequate food for day-to-day activities, which are quite energetic in young fish. The adult needs only sufficient amounts to sustain its basic needs and replace any tissues worn out by day-to-day activity.

Breeding fish of both sexes will consume more than normal rations. This is because they will be in a heightened state of excitement, and will therefore be more active. A fish recovering from an illness will also consume more food because it must replace tissue that was broken down to provide energy while it was ill and not feeding normally. A stressed fish may eat more, or less, than a normal one depending on how it reacts to that which is stressing it.

In the case where two or more piranhas are sharing an aquarium you must not overlook the possibility that one fish may not get its share of the food because its tank mate(s) prevent it from doing so. Even piranhas are subject to the social influence of their conspecifics—especially if these are larger or simply more aggressive.

To say that nutrition is a science is only a partial truth as any skilled aquarist will tell you. It is also an art inasmuch that it is highly dependent on the owner's ability to observe and take account of the many factors that influence fishes in general, and individuals in particular.

If feeder fishes are used in the diet remember that piranhas are rather messy and although they will kill their prey, they may not always eat every part of it. Part of the head or body may fall to the substrate and be ignored. Also, bits of flesh will be in suspension in the water, so it is essential that regular cleanings take place to reduce pollution and prevent water cloudiness.

THE SUBSTRATE, DECORATIONS & SETTING UP

When you establish an aquarium you are doing far more than providing a sort of a "cage" for your animals. You are creating an entire world for them. Every effort should be made to include in it those elements of the wild habitat that will enable your fishes to lead a healthy and very contented life.

You will need a gravel substrate, various rocks and bogwoods, and a selection of plants. The arrangement of these, called the aqua-scene, should be such that the piranha has an open swimming area, and an area into which it can retreat for shade as well as a sense of security when this is needed. Other than these basic requirements, you will want to obtain various accessories for the setting up of the aquarium, and thereafter for generally maintaining it.

These items will include one or two plastic buckets (never metal), one or more lengths of plastic tubing to use as a siphon, a gravel cleaner, a glass scraper to remove algae, a few small pots to hold plants, a planter, inert plant weights, plant foods, various water test kits, and a good hand lens. You can also purchase murals that can be placed on the back and side panels of the aquarium to conceal the wall, or whatever may be behind the tank (such as pieces of equipment).

Finally, with respect to decoration, you can construct a "stage" at the back of the aquarium on which you can include various items that will give the tank the illusion of having greater depth. If this appeals to you, you must allow for this when positioning the aquarium. Now that you have listed your needs in general, let us commence by discussing these in more detail, and how to set up the aquarium.

Serrasalmus gibbus **is called the "Golden Piranha" because of the golden color on its flanks and belly.**

PHOTO BY ANDRE ROTH

THE LOCATION

It is important that you choose the tank site with care. Very often this will mean a compromise that takes into account various factors.

1. The tank should be positioned such that it receives some natural daylight without being exposed to strong sunlight. The latter would interfere with the water temperature and encourage strong algal growth on the exposed panels. Piranhas do not like bright illumination.

2. It should not be where it will be subjected to cold drafts when doors are opened.

3. Avoid places where the human "traffic" is heavy and the fishes may be startled by the sudden appearance of a person. Stress created by this means can be a major precursor of illness. This is especially so with a piranha, which is actually a far more timid fish than you might think.

4. Select a site where it will be easy for you to service the aquarium with respect to partial water changes, cleaning, and general maintenance.

5. Avoid placing the unit close to heaters that will effect the temperature in the aquarium. As already discussed, rapid fluctuations in temperature is definitely a big negative where aquaria are concerned.

6. Choose a location where you can view your fishes with ease from the comfort of an armchair or sofa.

7. Double check that the location is well able to withstand the weight of the aquarium when it is filled with water. You can do this by stacking bricks or rocks of the same weight there, and spreading them over the same area that the tank will occupy.

THE SUBSTRATE

The floor of the tank should be covered with a layer of washed gravel that has a particle size of about one eighth of an inch. This provides a large enough surface area on which a good colony of beneficial bacteria can develop. If the substrate is of larger particle size it may provide pockets for uneaten food that will decay and increase pollution. If the particle size is too small it will be too fine for adequate water flow

Serrasalmus denticulatus from northwestern South America.

PHOTO BY ANDRE ROTH.

This fish acts like a piranha and schools with piranhas, but it might not be one; it hasn't been identified completely.

(and thus aeration) between the particles.

The depth should be about one inch at the front of the tank and rise to about three inches at the rear. This gradient promotes the accumulation of uneaten food and debris toward the front of the aquarium where it is more easily removed. Do not use any gravel that contains marble, oyster shell, or other calcium bearing material. You can utilize rocks or terraces to prevent the gravel from shifting toward the front of the tank.

ROCKS

As with the substrate, avoid using any calcium or metal bearing rocks—these would include marble, chalk, and dolomite. Over a span of time they will tend to make the water more alkaline and hard. Your best choices are granite, slate, basalt, lava, and hard sandstone. Choose an assortment of sizes from small through large, and those already smoothed by wear and with interesting shapes. You can purchase imitation rocks from your aquatic store. These look just like the real thing and are made from inert materials.

WOOD

This should be of the bogwood type, but never that which is rotting. This process consumes oxygen as a part of the decaying process. Woods that are not completely waterlogged will float, but you can weigh these down with rocks, or bind them with nylon string to a plastic base that is covered with gravel. You will never see the nylon string once a little algae has colonized the wood. As with rock, you can purchase synthetic woods shaped like branches, logs, and roots. These are heavier than water and totally safe to use.

PLANTS

A nice display of a few hardy plant species makes all the difference esthetically. All plants should be obtained from your aquarium dealer. Never gather them from the wild—you may inadvertently introduce pathogens to the aquarium. For piranhas, choose plants that are native to South America. These will include any of the broad leafed Amazon sword plants (genus *Echinodorus*). You need tall plants for the

rear and sides of the tank, with maybe one or two short specimen plants for the foreground.

Because the piranha is a large fish, you should not overstock the tank with plants, but feature enough to provide a natural look, and provide clumps of plants that the fish can retreat among. Plants can be very demanding with regard to lighting conditions. This is why it is best to restrict the choice to hardy specimens recommended by your dealer.

Obtain a suitable fertilizer, and be sure to trim off any dead or dying leaves both before and after they are placed in the aquarium. As an extra precaution against the risk of introducing bacteria into the water via the plants, it is suggested that they first be disinfected using one of the proprietary plant disinfectants.

SETTING UP YOUR AQUARIUM DISPLAY

Setting up a piranha tank will take quite a few hours, so be sure you have allowed enough time. It can be done in two stages, the first being preparatory, the second the actual setting up. It is useful to first make sketches of the aqua-scene you visualize. This will help you avoid obtaining too many or too few of the decorations you need. It is also easier to move things around on paper than when they are in the actual tank. The latter should be restricted to changes in details.

In planning the scene, try to make it look natural by not having it too symmetrical. Large rocks can be placed off-center, or at one end. Logs and slate can be used to create bridges or cave-like retreats. Any internal equipment or its tubing can be discreetly hidden behind rocks or stands of tall pants.

The first practical job will be to test the tank for leaks by filling it. This is best done in the kitchen, or even outdoors, where a leak will not cause too much damage. You can place about one cup of salt into the water per every 20 gallons. This will kill most bacteria. Leave this overnight, then empty the tank and flush it generously with

clean water. The tank can then be placed in position. Before doing this check to make sure that the surface is as flat as possible. If any unevenness, however minor, is detected you can place a cork or polystyrene mat under the tank. It is important that there is no area that is unsupported and which would be subject to excess stress.

Next, all equipment and decorations must be cleaned. In the case of the gravel you can place this in a bucket of water and insert a hose into it. Let this run until the water is clear of all signs of cloudiness. Stirring the gravel will help free stubborn dirt particles. If a mural is to be added to the rear glass, attend to this when the tank is clean and empty.

Now the actual setting up can be done using the following guidelines.

1. If an undergravel filter is to be featured its plate must be installed first. It is very important that the water cannot bypass the filter. To prevent this, the edges can be sealed using an aquarium sealant.

2. Place a layer of gravel over the filter plate, or the glass tank bottom as the case may be. You can then add a layer of plant fertilizer to the gravel. Alternatively, you can restrict this food locally to where the plants are being inserted, especially if they are to be contained in pots or plastic bags (which might be wise if an undergravel filter is to be used). The current of water passing through the gravel to a filter can unduly disturb the plant roots if it is too strong.

3. Place the large rocks in position, trying to avoid any pockets under them by filling these in with gravel. Especially avoid small cave-like gaps under the rocks into which pieces of uneaten meat may be carried by the current. Once they become trapped they will rot and pollute the tank.

4. Insert any terracing (this can be done initially if no filter plate is to be used).

5. Complete the substrate, sculpturing it to your needs.

6. Fill the tank to a depth about one third full. To avoid disturbing the substrate pour the water gently onto a plate or other suitable material.

7. Insert the plants and any food for them. The plants can be secured in the gravel using plant weights or if they are potted by covering the planting medium with gravel. It is easier to work with the plants if there is water in the aquarium. Their leaves will float and not be in your way, or at risk of being damaged as might be the case if you insert them into dry gravel.

8. Now you can add the heater and filter tubing (or the filter itself if it is internal). Be sure that the heater element is not in the gravel. This will create uneven heating and

11. Make initial water quality tests and make notes on these. Fit the cover glass and canopy to the aquarium. It is best to let the water reach room temperature before you switch on the heater. But all other equipment can now be plugged into electrical sockets to check and see that they are in working order. Once the water is at room temperature, the heater can be plugged in. Check very carefully that the heater(s) are performing correctly.

Although with modern water conditioners you can very quickly add one or two inexpensive fishes to the aquarium,

Serrasalmus gibbus is not a sensitive fish and lives well under aquarium conditions. They may jump out of their aquarium, so keep it covered.

there is a risk that the glass of the unit will crack or shatter. Do not switch on any electrical equipment while you are in the setting up stage—this could be dangerous, or even lethal to you, if it were faulty.

9. Place the external filter into position, along with the air pump, if one is being used.

10. Fill the aquarium to about 1-2 inches from the top. Add water conditioners to remove the chlorine and chloramines. Now is the time to use your long-handled planter to make any minor changes in the plant arrangement. If you wish, you can add nitrogen cycle starter cultures, or small slithers of meat on a string, so the needed bacterial colonies can be encouraged to start.

it is wise to wait at least two weeks before adding a piranha. This gives the water at least some time to mature and build up the bacterial colony needed to convert the nitrites to nitrates. It can take months to build up a large bacterial colony in a large aquarium.

You will find, initially, that the nitrite reading will fluctuate considerably, so you must wait until it has peaked and dropped and is constantly at zero or very close to this. Likewise, the pH reading will vary depending on the time of day the water is tested, so do this at the same time of day on a regular schedule.

If the pH or hardness levels are not as required you can obtain resins from your

dealer to adjust these to desired values. Peat in the filters will increase acidity, chalk in it will increase hardness.

ADDING THE PIRANHA

Only when the water conditions are just right, and especially only when the temperature is constant at about 77°F should you purchase and introduce the piranha. There are three things to take into consideration. First the bag in which the piranha was transported (if it was a bag) should be floated on the surface to let its water temperature equate with that of the aquarium water. Next you should carefully open the neck of the bag and allow some tank water into it so that the fish gets a "feeling" for the new water. Finally, you can open the bag completely and let the fish swim gently into the tank. The whole process can take from 20-40 minutes. Do not "pour" the fish into the tank. This will stress it badly. It may panic and damage itself against the glass or rocks.

You are cautioned in all of your dealings with these fishes that while most of them will not be aggressive, all of them can inflict dangerous bites, so must be handled with the greatest respect at all times. Of course, very young fish of two inches or less will hardly be able to inflict more than a tiny bite, but you should learn to respect them from the outset.

ROUTINE CLEANING

Once the aquarium is up and running it must be routinely attended. This means removing debris from the tank, cleaning the filters, and removing excess algae from the viewing glass, rocks, and equipment. Test the water on a regular basis—minor fluctuations in pH and hardness will not be a problem, but those related to nitrates are indicative of whether or not the nitrogen cycle is being effected adequately.

Partial water changes should be made every 21 days or so at which time 25% of the water can be exchanged. Be sure to heat the added water so that it is at the required

Serrasalmus denticulatus are dangerous in many ways. Submergible heaters with cables loose in the water are in danger of being bitten by piranhas.

PHOTO BY DR. HERBERT R. AXELROD

This species has been sold as a piranha. When it starts eating plants instead of other fishes, you know it's not a piranha!

temperature before it is placed in the aquarium.

SAFETY PRECAUTIONS

There are two safety considerations. One is related to the electricity, the other to the piranha. Never (!) place your hands into water while the electrical equipment is plugged into a socket. With respect to the fish, it is wise not to risk getting bitten, even though your piranha is apparently placid.

One way to work at chores in the tank, and do so safely, is to obtain a sheet of Plexiglas the width and height of the tank and drill a number of small holes into it (the holes allow it to be moved in the aquarium with greater ease). It should be tall enough that the fish cannot swim over it. By using this as a divider you can restrict the fish's movement so that you can reach into the aquarium without any risk that your pet will decide to try and snack on your arm or bite your fingers, or nip at them in fright. The alternative is, of course, to remove the piranha to a smaller holding tank. This is the way to proceed when a major cleaning job is to be undertaken.

As for the actual catching process, nets must be avoided as these fish can easily bite holes in them. In any case, rough nets may also damage the piranha's scales and fins. The gentlest, and safest, way to move a piranha from one tank to another is by the use of a plastic trap or bucket into which the fish is herded using a small net.

In the event a piranha of reasonable size should somehow flip out of a bucket, exercise extreme care when recovering it. When flipping on a carpet a piranha will panic and bite madly at anything and everything. Place an empty bucket near them and as gently as possibly scoop them into this, quickly adding some aquarium water.

THE TRUTH ABOUT WILD PIRANHAS

The piranha is hardly alone among animals that have gained fearsome reputations as being the most dangerous creatures in their domains. Consider gorillas, sharks, wolves, snakes, tarantulas, and tigers, just to name a few. Few animals are as timid and retiring as gorillas, and most sharks would flee, or show little more than curiosity, at the sight of a human. The reliably documented accounts of wolves attacking humans could be counted on the fingers of one hand, while only a few snakes represent any threat to humans—and these commonly only attack when provoked or startled.

This is not to say that the piranha and the other creatures mentioned are not dangerous. It is simply that their danger has been blown out of all proportion. News reporters, together with TV and movie producers, are little concerned with things that are not regarded as especially dangerous in the day-to-day lives of people who live with these creatures. That doesn't sell their products. However, if a fish that most people know nothing about can strip a man to bare bones in seconds, now that is something else!

Matters are certainly exacerbated if a well respected person states that this or that animal is highly dangerous to humans and all others it comes into contact with. Never mind if that person never actually studied the animal's habits to establish any basis for the believed facts he or she was stating. Once a legend has been built, it can be very difficult to dispel, especially if there is in fact an element of truth on which that legend has been based. This is the case with piranhas.

THE RISKY LIFE OF THE PIRANHA

The first way to bring perspective to the truth about a piranha is to look at certain realities concerning its own ability to survive in the wild. If these fishes were indeed such ferocious killers it would follow that there would be few other fishes or other creatures living in waters where it abounds. It would have hunted them out of existence, in which case, by now, most piranhas would then have eaten each other! The fact that hundreds of other fish species live in the same waters as piranhas would strongly suggest that these fishes are successful enough in avoiding being eaten so that the piranha is unable to decimate their populations.

The piranha is not a predator that reigns over its domain with impunity. It is itself a prey species to many other animals that live in the same waters—such is the complex web of life. Granted, it is a prime predator, much as the lion and tiger are, but they, too, have no "golden passport" to survival in their domain.

If the largest of the piranhas were to carelessly pass in front of the jaws of a waiting crocodile or caiman, it would quickly find its reputation meant nothing to these animals! It would rapidly be just another morsel to these reptiles. Every year many thousands of piranhas end up as meals to these creatures.

Similar numbers end up in the bellies of river dolphins, while even more thousands fall prey to river turtles and otters. Otters! But aren't these mammals like us? That's right, and there are other non-fish or non-reptile species that have no aversion to taking a few piranhas as a meal, including large herons, eagles, and other fish-eating birds.

Now if this isn't bad enough for the piranha, most of its own prey species will actually decimate the piranhas before they become large enough to eat their prey. Millions of piranha eggs and fry will never live for more time than it takes for some quite small fishes to come along and gobble them up, just another snack in their own quest for food.

So, getting by as an adult piranha can be

PHOTO BY HARALD SCHULTZ.

This Karaja indian caught this *Serrasalmus nattereri* for his dinner.

quite difficult at the best of times, and the odds are heavily stacked against it reaching maturity in the first place. If you then add to the equation the hundreds of thousands that are caught each year by native fishermen, the piranha needs all of its ferocity and reputation in order to hold its own within its domain! It must also be born in mind that its prey species don't just stay put and allow themselves to be eaten. Some are much faster swimmers than the piranha, and quickly put distance between themselves and the piranha (or a school of them). The prey, too, usually have very sensitive detection devices and can detect schools of predators (piranhas) moving toward them in the water.

Other fish species, when approached by a piranha on a one-to-one basis, will turn toward it and stand their ground. When this happens the piranha may have "second thoughts" about attacking—much as an individual lion is easily dissuaded from attacking a water buffalo that turns to face it.

The result of these realities is that the piranha has to really work hard to survive— just like all the other inhabitants of the rivers and lakes in which it lives. A balanced equilibrium is thus maintained.

THE THREAT TO HUMANS

The foregoing should have dispelled the notion that the piranha is anything more than just another of life's problems to most creatures that share its domain. The piranha is to them just another threat and/or just another potential meal. As a threat it is no more dangerous than a crocodile, a dolphin, a turtle, an otter, a bird, a snake, or any of hundreds of other animals that will make a meal of them if the opportunity arises. Some fish species are even more at risk to certain of these animals, or to other fish species, such as catfishes, than they are to the piranha.

This brings us to the threat to humans by these undeniably dangerous fishes. There is an infinitely higher risk that a piranha will be killed by a human than there is of a human being killed by a piranha. There is a much higher risk that a human will be killed, or mauled, in piranha infested waters by other fish species, reptiles, or mammals, than there is from direct danger at the mouths of these fishes. In terms of hard facts, your chances of being attacked by something in the jungles or rain forests of South America are such that you would be safer swimming with the piranhas than staying on land! Each year hundreds of South American natives are killed by venomous snakes—but documented evidence of deaths by piranhas is almost impossible to come by.

It must, however, be conceded that if a school of piranhas did attack a human there would be little evidence to document! It is this little word "if" that is enough to perpetuate the legend of the piranha. Even the most knowledgeable expert on these fishes would not be foolish enough to state that there would be no risk to a human entering piranha infested waters.

It comes down more to a case of the odds against a person being attacked, and under what conditions would these odds start to change such that one would be very well advised not to take them. The chances of a human being attacked are remote at best. There are sound reasons for this. Mammals generally, and humans especially, are not aquatic, thus not among the normal prey species of these fishes. As a result, a piranha has better things to do with its time than to be unduly concerned by the sight of a human in water. Like most sharks, lions, or other creatures, it may show interest in a human because it cannot be sure how secure its own life is. It is able to detect that the human is larger than itself, and thus may be dangerous—so it will keep its distance. It will check the odors and the sound waves (pressure waves) for any indications of distress or blood. If these are not evident it will move on looking for more easy-to-take natural prey whose habits it is far more familiar with.

HOW THE ODDS CHANGE

The river-bank natives of piranha habitats know when it is and isn't safe to enter the water. They know the piranha will become excited by the smell of blood, and that this

PHOTO BY LEO NICO AND DONALD TAPHORN.

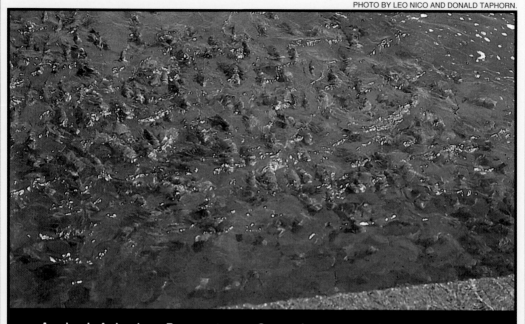

A school of piranhas, *Pygocentrus* or *Serrasalmus notatus* in a feeding frenzy.

will attract any piranhas lurking in the immediate vicinity. They know that if an animal or fish is in distress it will thrash about in the water, and that this, too, will attract these fishes. And they know that certain parts of a river may be favorite hunting grounds for piranhas. These fishes will tend to congregate at such places. It is likely that they will be making regular kills there, so will often be in an excited state.

They know that if a stretch of water has dried out or has become cut off from its main flow, the piranha will exhaust the water of prey fishes, and eventually become very hungry. This will drive them to be less cautious and to be more likely to "test bite" any potentially edible item.

Under these conditions one or more of the more bold piranhas will approach ever closer, then eventually snap at the human. Once the first bite is taken and blood is flowing, the school will go into its feeding frenzy. Its natural fear or disinterest of the human will instantly vanish. Once this state is reached, unless the human is in very shallow water, the chances of him or her coming out alive would be all but zero, depending, of course, on how many piranhas were present.

The natives have ascertained all of these facts over many years. They may never have seen a person killed in piranha infested waters, but they were educated from the cradle that these realities were truths handed down to them by their parents, and to them by their parents, and so on. They see sufficient evidence of these truths in their daily lives——partially consumed fishes, baited meat, or bites on other natives from the careless handling of a netted piranha.

They and their children can swim and thrash without concern in the shallow waters near their village. They know that as long as they do not have open wounds the piranha may come, but will then go away again when no scent of blood or sense of distress is established. So regular are these routines that the piranha will ultimately not even bother to come too close.

When crossing deeper stretches of rivers the natives will do so slowly and without attracting undue attention to themselves, though wide and deep rivers will normally only be crossed via canoe—why push your luck!

A head on view of a young *Serrasalmus nattereri*. His teeth are always showing and his eyes are pitched in such a way that he has binocular vision, a rare characteristic among fishes. Most of them can only focus both eyes on objects in a distance.

From the foregoing you will see that these fishes are no more dangerous to a human than is the crocodile that will lay basking along the banks of the same rivers, or the anaconda that may be swimming in the river, or the stingray that lays motionless on the sandy substrate. That it is capable of accomplishing everything its evil reputation tells us it can is not in dispute. It is the likelihood of it doing so to the average informed traveler of regions where it lives is where the truth has been bent and twisted to the degree it has formed a circle!

For all of the truths given in this discussion, the piranha will still maintain its place as one of the most feared animals we can think of. The reason is that with most other animals having similar notorious reputations, we also believe that there would be some chance we could avoid death. Maybe a stick would keep them at bay, or we might have a gun, or could climb a tree—or maybe even jump into a river. But if piranhas attacked in numbers there simply would be no chance of escape and survival. That is a sobering truth!

BREEDING PIRANHAS

The breeding of piranhas is still very much in its infancy, since only a few species having been bred, and these usually in the very large tanks of public aquariums. The species bred so far are *S. spilopleura*, *S. gibbus*, *S. rhombeus*, and possibly *Pygocentrus nattereri*.

The reasons for this dearth of success are not surprising. Any attempts to breed these fishes should not even be contemplated unless one has a tank of at least 100-300-gallon capacity. This immediately places breeding well out of the reach of the average aquarist. There is then the fact that the sexes, with but one exception, are not readily identifiable externally. This means that a number of them must be kept in order to try and discern, by behavior patterns, which are possibly a true pair.

Even having obtained a pair and supplying them with a large enough aquarium, it has to be hoped that they will be compatible. This is by no means certain. Some time may also be required (which may be a year or two) before they are ready to reproduce, and only then if all conditions are to their liking.

Finally, even if a pair spawned it would be a costly undertaking to raise even a few of these to maturity unless you had more large tanks for rearing purposes. Piranha fry, even a few days old, are quite ferocious toward their siblings, and have no qualms in adding them to their daily menu. If other adults are sharing the same tank, these too will soon devour the youngsters. Given these rather depressing realities, the following information will complete your knowledge on these fishes, and provide some data and hints for those who are in a position to attempt to breed their piranhas.

Hiroshi Azuma stunned the aquarium world with his spawning of *Serrasalmus nattereri* in Japan many years ago. He lost many females when they became egg-bound. By dissecting them, Azuma found thousands of small, ripe eggs.

PHOTO BY HIROSHI AZUMA

EGGLAYING

Piranhas are oviparous fishes, meaning they are egglayers, the eggs hatching outside of their body. Even within this method of reproduction there are different techniques used to ensure that a percentage of the eggs survive and develop into fry. Some species are egg scatterers, the currents taking the eggs away from the parents who would otherwise eat them.

Some fishes are egg buriers, placing their eggs in the substrate. Some are egg depositors, carefully fixing the eggs to plants or rocks where they are guarded by the parents. Piranhas are in the group known as nest-builders, though there are scatterers among them as well. The former prepare rough nests from leaves or depressions they make in the substrate. Here the eggs are laid and guarded by one or both parents—predominantly the male. This care of the eggs and fry seems rather out of place, given the ferocity of these fishes. But those piranhas that do defend their offspring do so with the same level of aggression that they show in their day to day predatory lives.

In spite of this parental care, if other fishes share the same tank, which is not advisable with breeding pairs, many eggs and fry will be eaten while they are still very small and unable to defend themselves, which they surely will do once they have reached a few inches in length.

BREEDING PREPARATION

Before piranhas can be bred they must be in superb physical condition—well fed, contented, and stress-free in their accommodations. They are thus best kept in pairs so that there are no other fishes to bother them.

Inducing breeding is not yet fully understood, it being more a case of "if you see the signs they must be ready." Raising the temperature a few degrees may help induce spawning, as may the addition of a little fresh water. A pair will commonly

The breeding pair of *Serrasalmus nattereri* prepare to spawn by clearing the area. They move the small stones and chew up the vegetation to make a suitable spawning nest.

Once the breeding pair of *Serrasalmus nattereri* have prepared their spawning site, they rub against each other and release huge quantities of eggs.

swim together and the male will probably start to display a darkening of his colors in a very short time span. The pair will commence nest preparations by biting away pieces of vegetation, moving small rocks, and fashioning a depression at a chosen site. It is therefore essential that they have suitable plants, which should include those that will readily hold the eggs, such as Java moss, or peat in which depressions can be made. The male will drive the female around the tank in an effort to guide her to the nesting area. He may take pieces from her fins (and body), and vice versa, so courtship in these fishes is conducted at much the same level of violence as most other aspects of their lives!

Eventually, she will come to rest in the spawning area and he will approach her from the side in order to fertilize as many of her eggs as he can. This ritual will be repeated a number of times until all the eggs are shed.

EGGS AND THEIR CARE

The number of eggs laid is very variable, but within the range of 700-4,000. They are deposited as a sticky mass so that they will retain their position in the nest (if of this type). Alternatively, the egg scattering species, such as *S. gibbus*, will simply deposit their eggs at random around the spawning area.

If egg scattering is observed, it would be wise to remove the parents as chances are they will readily eat them (and fry if the eggs ever get to hatch). In fact, even with parents that protect their eggs it may be prudent, with a first spawning, to do likewise, or to remove most of the eggs to a safe place for hatching. This is in case the parents become nervous and decide to devour their brood. At the next spawning you could always allow them to look after most, or even all, of their offspring to see how things go.

It is advised that you treat the water with a suitable disinfectant, such as methylene blue, from your pet shop so as to minimize the risk of fungus attacking the eggs. However, this usually happens only to the eggs that are infertile, the healthy ones usually proving very resistant to fungus and parasites, assuming that the water is clean and not polluted.

If eggs are hatched away from the main tank the suggested initial temperature is 77°F, which should be raised by 3-4 degrees when the eggs hatch.

REARING THE FRY

Once the eggs hatch, which will be anytime after 2-9 days depending on the species and the water temperature, the fry will soon begin feeding on newly hatched brine shrimp. They rapidly progress to small worms, and if not given enough food, they will just as rapidly attack each other!

It is essential, in order to minimize cannibalism, that each fry has at least one gallon of water—thus 50 fry will need a minimum tank size of 50 gallons. In reality, because of the numbers of fry that hatch, and the speed with which they grow— about 2.5cm (1in) a month—it is almost inevitable that within the average hobbyists' tanks most will perish for one reason or another, usually due to lack of space and/ or food.

After about five months the growth rate starts to slow down a little, and by eight to ten months most are losing, or have lost,

A close-up of *Serrasalmus nattereri* eggs which adhere to the spawning substrata. The developing embryos are clearly visible. Most of the thousands of eggs released by the female were successfully fertilized by the male.

PHOTO BY HIROSHI AZUMA

A two-week old embryo of *Serrasalmus nattereri* with its yolk sac almost entirely absorbed. The fry is about 1 cm in length (there are 2.54 cm to an inch).

their juvenile coloration. These remarks are of course based on just the few species in which breeding has been observed, so it remains to be seen if what has just been said is reasonably typical for the genus as a whole.

Once a spawning has taken place, the pair may spawn again within two or three weeks, but this may prove to be an unwanted happening if you already have one batch of fry that you are trying to raise.

KEEPING RECORDS

Given the scarcity of breeding reports within this group of fishes every spawning is something of an achievement. This being so, it behooves breeders to maintain diligent records of any successful spawnings so that this can be disseminated among other breeders. The sort of data that should be recorded is as follows:

Observations on behavioral patterns that preceded courtship.

Color changes in the fish.

Water conditions.

Plants and other decorations in the aquarium.

Age of parents (if known) and their size.

How long they had been together, and were others in the same tank.

Observations on the placement of eggs and any nests that were prepared.

Hatching time.

Foods supplied.

Growth rate.

Notes on behavior of the fry, and the development of their colors and markings.

This information can be supplied to hobbyists through clubs as well as through articles that can be offered to aquarium magazines or scientific journals.

THE PIRANHA SPECIES

Before discussing the various piranha species you are likely to choose from, there are three other subjects that will be of interest to you. These relate to the legality of owning any of these fishes, your responsibility to your pet, and the derivation of the name piranha.

PIRANHAS—THEIR LEGAL STATUS

Before purchasing a piranha you are advised to check its legal standing in both your state and area. Many states forbid the ownership of these fishes. Even where they may be kept statewide there may be local ordinances that forbid them. The reason is that in the federal and state departments there is a fear that if these fishes were to be released into local rivers or lakes they might become established, thus have a devastating effect on indigenous species. There is also the perceived danger to humans.

Such releases are most likely from people trying to dispose of unwanted pets. Now you might think that pet owners would never do this—sadly you would be very wrong. Within all pet hobbies there are a small number of people who should never be allowed to own any animal. They are totally irresponsible, uncaring, and move from one pet to another on a fanciful whim. They are the scourge of pet hobbies. They are the sort that dump dogs, cats, potbellied pigs, and other pets into local parks to get rid of them. They also release unwanted cage birds, and will release surplus stocks of fishes into ponds and rivers. While the chances of a few released piranhas being able to establish populations in habitats alien to them is remote in the extreme, it would be equally irresponsible of serious hobbyists to say this could not be possible. Wild populations of non–indigenous species of fishes, birds, and mammals residing now in the USA, and other countries, are testimony to this fact.

A PIRANHA OWNER'S RESPONSIBILITY

Before you even purchase a piranha you should carefully examine your reasons for wanting one. If it is to impress friends, or simply to watch it devour defenseless fishes, these are very poor reasons and the desired effect will not last long. As a responsible owner you should consider the reality that the small youngster(s) you obtain will soon become much larger, and will cost more to feed. If you are not prepared to invest a substantially larger sum of money into relocating them in a large tank, what will you do with them? Do not assume that a public aquarium or a pet shop will be prepared to take them from you—even at no cost.

If these outlets are not interested in your now-too-large piranha, you must be prepared to contact tropical fish clubs to see if they have members who will take the fish. This is entirely possible. However, if all these avenues fail, the only(!) responsible option left is to have your vet painlessly destroy the fish.

Do not think that releasing them into the wild is being considerate toward your pet. This is ducking responsibility. Such a released piranha would be doomed to a miserable existence that can only end in starvation, illness, and slow death, unless another predator devoured it, which is eventually what would probably happen.

THE NAME "PIRANHA"

The common name of this group of species has its derivation in the languages used by South American Indians that have known the fish as long as they have had a language. Their own languages have been subject to hybridization resulting from the effect of successive waves of other Indian tribes that have invaded them, and by words introduced by Spanish and Portuguese colonists. Locally, piranhas are known

Various fishes have been sold as piranhas. Here are some which are NOT piranhas and are not dangerous:
1. The Hatchetfish, *Carnegiella marthae* prefers eating small insects. 2. *Piaractus brachypomum* really looks like a piranha, but it isn't. 3. A full grown *Colossoma macropomum*. 4. *Colossoma macropomum* juvenile. 5. *Mylossoma paraguayensis* is a vegetarian. 6. *Mylossoma duriventre* is a vegetable eating fish. It doesn't eat other fishes. 7. *Mylossoma aureum* is a vegetarian as are all *Mylossoma*. 8. *Mylossoma aureum* juvenile.
All of these fishes can be kept in the same aquarium but they will eat live plants so only use plastic plants, rocks and safe driftwood.

under many different names according to the habits of the fishes, dangerous or less so, and by their colors.

Let us start with the correct pronunciation. It is not "peranna" as most English speaking people will say it. It should be pronounced "Pee-rrahn'-ya", with the accent on the "rahn" and a rolled "r", though few English speaking people can roll the "r" as do the Spanish and Portuguese.

In the general hybrid Amazonian language of patois spoken by many natives, and derived from the Tupi tribe, pira means a fish. Rahna, tanha and sanha, depending on locality, mean tooth. Thus the Pira-rahna is the toothed fish, and when shortened by the English it became piranha.

However, some early explorers translated it as meaning "scissors" fish, overlooking the fact that these appliances were probably named for the fish, not the reverse. When the first Indians saw scissors the cutting action reminded them of the teeth of these fishes, so scissors came to be known as piranha. Historically, and to this day, the teeth of these fish were in fact used for various cutting tools by the Indians, so the early error by explorers is easy to understand.

Without going into all of their derivations, the following are just some of the other names used in South American countries for these fishes, some of which indicate whether they refer to those known to be dangerous, or those regarded as not so dangerous. You may see them appearing from time to time in the literature.

Caribe: Venezuela. Dangerous species. Named for the Carib Indian tribe, a very cruel tribe of marauding conquerors.

Chupita: Brazil. Dangerous species.

Pacu: Non dangerous piranhas and related species.

Palometa: Bolivia and Uruguay. Dangerous species, though the term means "little dove." The word piranha in these countries is, ironically, applied to the less dangerous species.

Pana: Peru.

Perai or Pirai: Guyana. The most dangerous species.

Piraya. Brazil. A corruption of piranha used in certain areas.

Pirambeba. North and Eastern Brazil. Non dangerous species.

Piranha-verdadeira: Brazil. The true dangerous piranha.

Rodoleira: Brazil. General name.

Umati: Brazil. Indian name for piranha.

THE SPECIES

Exactly how many species of piranha there are is open to much debate in zoological circles. This is because some species have been labeled such on no more than color and size differences, and are based on limited numbers of specimens. Large numbers of specimens are fundamental to any authoritative classification. It is always possible, as has been illustrated in fishes, birds, and other animal groups, that what was considered for a long time to be a species was no more than an immature example that displayed juvenile size and color differences. Piranhas show a tremendous range of colors, which change as they mature, so errors from this aspect are easy to make.

Sexually dimorphic examples (where the sexes are distinguished on the basis of external appearance) have also been labeled as different species, as have geographic color variants. It is therefore entirely possible that some of the following species may at some future date be found to be one and the same. It is also quite probable that some species remain to be identified and described scientifically. Others listed may prove yet to be subspecies.

The subgeneric status of these fishes has been ignored here because this taxon is invariably changed continually by taxonomists. The species are arranged alphabetically rather than by distribution (as is normal) so you can more readily refer to them.

Sizes are maximum approximates for mature specimens, head and body only (without tail). A number of species have no common names as they are not as yet well known enough in the hobby to have been given

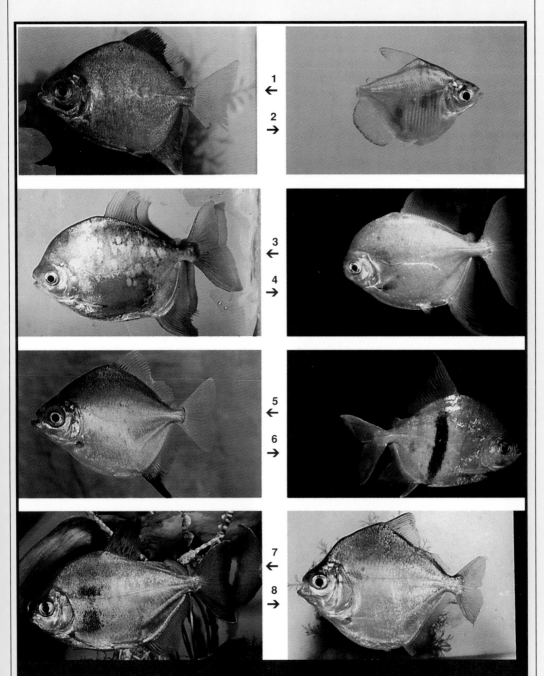

These fishes are usually sold as piranhas, but now that the importation of piranhas is banned in most civilized countries, the tables have turned and the piranhas are now called by non-piranha names on export documents. 1. *Myleus pacu* is the name of this so-called metynnis. The name *pacu* is the indian name used in Brazil. 2. *Myleus micans*. 3. and 4.*Myleus rubripinnis*. This may be the most popular of the *Myleus*. 5. *Myleus ternetzi*. 6. *Myleus schomburgki* is the most expensive of the *Myleus*. 7. *Metynnis argenteus*. 8. *Metynnis luna*.

them. Common names have no scientific standing anyway, becoming established solely by convention of their use.

The name following the species name is its author and following that is the date the species was first described. If the author's name is in parentheses this indicates that the species was originally placed in another genus.

Descriptive text, other than for color and markings, has been restricted to those species you are likely to be able to obtain and where the species is well documented and therefore of interest to hobbyists.

There are currently four genera of "piranhas" (*Pristobrycon*, *Pygocentrus*, *Pygopristis*, and *Serrasalmus*), with a fifth (*Catoprion*) generally included with the group by aquarists although not a true piranha. However, the piranhas are undergoing a revision and no doubt their classification will undergo many changes before it is finished. For that reason, even though scientists have generally accepted the breakdown of the genus *Serrasalmus* into the genera mentioned in the text, aquarists still use the name for all of the piranhas, which is reflected in the captions.

Catoprion mento (Cuvier, 1819) Wimple or Winged piranha

Venezuela, Guianas, Brazil, Bolivia. 14cm (5.5in). Although not in the genera of true piranhas, the wimple (meaning banner) piranha has become progressively more popular with aquarists. It rarely exceeds 10cm (4in), but its fin-nipping habits mean that it's best kept in a single species tank.

It is named for the elongated rays of its anterior dorsal and anal fins. Color is silvery with a red opercular spot, a black base to the caudal fin, and brick red in the anal fin. The species breeds well in captivity.

Pristobrycon aureus (Spix in Agassiz, 1829) Golden piranha.

Venezuela, Brazil. 36cm (14in). Caribe dorado = savage gold. Color is an iridescent mixture of olive and gold, the body covered with very small dark spots. Not regarded as an especially dangerous species, it is nevertheless not popular.

Pristobrycon calmoni (Steindachner, 1908) Dusky piranha

Brazil. 23cm (9in). The dorsal area of this rather bland piranha is gray to black. A dark blotch present behind gills. Some red in the anal fin. Body is silvery with faint black spots. Occasionally available, but not popular.

Pristobrycon striolatus (Steindachner, 1908)

Venezuela, Guyana. The profile suggests a non dangerous species. Color is dark above, sides silvery, and red into the paired and anal fins. The base of the tail is black banded.

Pygocentrus cariba (Humboldt, in Humboldt & Valenciennes, 1821) Red-bellied piranha

Venezuela, Brazil. 25cm (10in). This is another species that is somewhat similar to *P. nattereri*, which also has the common name red-bellied piranha applied to it. It is also an aggressive and somewhat unpredictable fish in an aquarium. Its distinctive shoulder spot and more fiery red color should help differentiate it from its much more popular cousin. *P. notatus* is a synonym.

Pygocentrus nattereri (Kner), 1860 Red Piranha, Red-bellied Piranha, Natterer's Piranha

Venezuela, Guiana, Brazil, Paraguay. 25cm (10in). The mature *P. nattereri* has a silvery iridescent body richly speckled with green-blue. The throat and underbelly are red of varying intensities, while the nape is grayish. In contrast, juveniles are not unlike *S. hollandi* with their spotted bodies. Colors vary greatly as the species matures.

These are all fishes of the genus *Catoprion*. There are three species. The usual species with the relatively shorter anal and dorsal fins is called *Catoprion mento*. It was first described in 1819. Dr. Axelrod described *Catoprion* "Geryi" from the Mato Grosso. It looks like *Catoprion mento* except the fish has a double longest ray in the dorsal and anal fins. A third species from the Pantanal of the Rio Paraguay drainage has extremely long dorsal and anal fins and Dr. Axelrod has called this *Catoprion* "Paraguayensis".

The adult bulldog-like build indicates quite clearly that this is a dangerous fish, possibly the most dangerous for its size in its wild habitat. It is also by far the most popular in the aquarium hobby, being much smaller than the similar looking piraya. It is a well-established breeder in aquaria.

Pygocentrus piraya (Cuvier, 1819)
Brazil. 53cm (21in). This very large piranha is dark-colored, ranging from Olive-brown to almost black, but with uneven silvery spots showing through and some red under the throat. It is definitely one of the most dangerous species, requiring a very large tank with very few companions! Not popular.

Pygocentrus ternetzi Steindachner, 1908
Paraguay, Argentina. 25cm (10in). Similar to *P. nattereri*, and may even wind up being a synonym of that species, but current thought is that the southern populations should be considered a valid species (*P. ternetzi*). It is another of the dangerous species in its natural habitat.

Pygopristis antoni Fernandez-Yepez, 1965
Venezuela. Caribe palometa = savage dove. Basic color silvery with black spots on the dorsal area. Some red in the paired fins and lower jaw, also in the anal fin. Now considered a possible synonym of *P. denticulatus*.

Pygopristis denticulatus (Cuvier, 1819)
Venezuela, Guianas, Brazil. 20cm (8in). Caribe palometa = Savage dove. This species has a silver color with some faint dark spots. The paired fins are yellow through red, this becoming a dark ochre to red with a black ending on the large anal fin. Not a highly dangerous species, nevertheless it should be treated with great respect. Its teeth are five cusped. The male of this species has a pronounced extension of the anterior rays of the anal fin when compared to that of the female—assuming this fin is fully intact, which is not always the case with this group of fishes.

Serrasalmus altuvei Ramírez, 1965.
Venezuela. Caribe azul = savage blue. The back is well humped, the lower jaw more upturned. Color silvery with some blue on flanks. Pinkish hues on underbelly. Dark vertical markings

Serrasalmus brandtii Reinhardt in Lütken, 1874
Brazil. This silver piranha with some yellow and brown in the anal and paired fins, is one of the non-dangerous species. The tell-tale signs are the large eyes, the less pronounced mouth, the smaller (but still very sharp) teeth, and the slim, compressed body.

Serrasalmus eigenmanni Norman, 1928
Venezuela, Guyana. The upper body is a mixture of olive and steel blue, the flanks being silver changing to white on the underbelly. Breeding pairs, as in a number of species, become much darker in color. Some red in paired, and anal fins. Upper body sports large dark spots. Although said to be non dangerous, it is better regarded as midway between the two types. Body rhomboid.

Serrasalmus elongatus Kner, 1860 Pike piranha
Venezuela, Brazil. 25cm (10in). This species is one of the least piranha shaped, being rather elongated. The color is basically all silver. It is a scale or fin nipper of larger fishes, but will of course attack and swallow smaller species. It is within the "non dangerous to humans" category.

Serrasalmus gibbus Castelnau, 1855 Golden piranha
Brazil, Peru. 31cm (12in). Named for the golden color of its flanks and underbelly, the dorsal surface is dark, being shades of blue. As with most piranhas, there is an iridescence to the scales. It is a dangerous species occasionally available to aquarists. Possibly a synonym of *S. rhombeus* (Linnaeus, 1766).

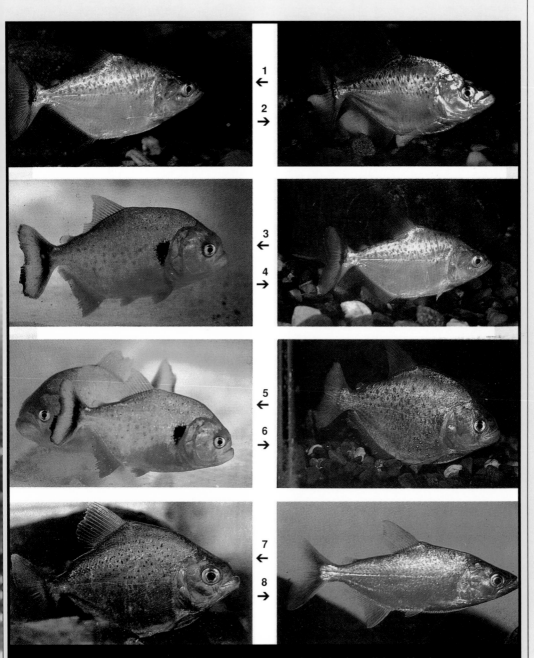

These are all REAL piranhas. They are dangerous both in the wild and in the aquarium. They do not attack humans in nature unless they are starving. In the aquarium they attack your hand because they are threatened. 1. *Serrasalmus eigenmanni*. 2. *Serrasalmus eigenmanni*. 3. *Serrasalmus notatus*. 4. *Serrasalmus eigenmanni*. 5. *Serrasalmus notatus*. 6. An unidentified *Serrasalmus*. 7. *Serrasalmus striolatus*. 8. *Serrasalmus elongatus*.

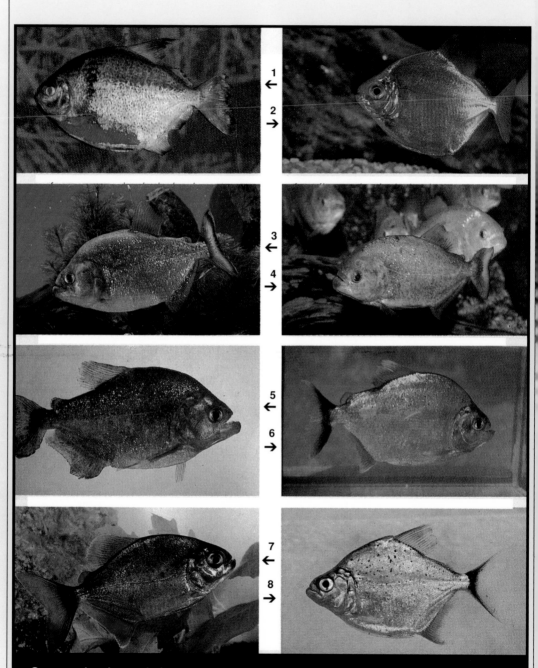

Some real and some imitators. 1. *Metynnis maculatus* is a very attractive fish with what looks like a red gash on its belly. This is strictly a plant-eater. 2. *Metynnis hypsauchen*. 3. *Serrasalmus gibbus* is a dangerous piranha. 4. *Serrasalmus sanchezi*. 5. *Serrasalmus spilopleura*. 6. *Serrasalmus antoni*. 7. *Serrasalmus denticulatus*. 8. *Serrasalmus striolatus* which looks like a *Metynnis* but has the teeth of a piranha.

A group of the rarely seen piranhas include many of the common ones but from hard-to-reach areas. *Serrasalmus nattereri* is a very variable piranha which soon should be separated into a dozen species when some aggressive splitter studies them. 1. *Serrasalmus elongatus* is a lake species which is very elongated. 2. *Serrasalmus hollandi.* 3. *Serrasalmus nattereri*, a juvenile. 4. *Serrasalmus nattereri*, sub-adult. 5. *Serrasalmus manueli.* 6. *Serrasalmus nattereri*, an adult. 7. *Serrasalmus rhombeus*, so named because of its shape. 8. *Serrasalmus serrulatus.*

Serrasalmus hollandi Eigenmann, 1915
Holland's piranha

Brazil. 15cm (6in). Being one of the smaller species, *S. hollandi* is suited to the aquarium hobby more than most species. It is in the non dangerous category. The ground color is silver to blue-brown, depending on the light reflections. There are distinctive dark spots of varying intensity. Some red in the fins, most noticeably in the anal. Tail almost transparent, with a dark base. Will become very dark in color with age—and when breeding. The shape is not unlike that of *S. rhombeus*.

Serrasalmus nalseni Fernandez-Yepez, 1969

Venezuela. This species is another of those that feature dark spots on its body. With red in its fins time may prove it is not a good species but a synonym of an earlier named species.

Serrasalmus niger (Schomburgk in Jardine, 1864)
Black piranha

Venezuela, Guianas. 36cm (14in). Although this large dark to black piranha has a much more unsavory reputation than *S. rhombeus*, it is considered to be the same species by some authorities. It is also regarded as being very unpredictable in its nature when kept in aquaria, so it is not very popular.

Serrasalmus nigricans Agassiz in Spix & Agassiz, 1829

Brazil. 25cm (10in). Somewhat similar to *P. nattereri*, but smaller and lacking red on the body and in the fins.

Serrasalmus pingke Fernandez-Yepez, 1951

Venezuela. This piranha has an elongate body and is considered a synonym of *S. elongatus*. It is called caribe pinche, meaning minion.

Serrasalmus rhombeus (Linnaeus, 1766)
White piranha, Spotted piranha

Venezuela, Guyana, Brazil. 46cm (18 in). This very large piranha is easily distinguished from *S. hollandi* by its larger size, the caudal and ventral fin colors, these being black edged in this species, and by the larger number of dark spots covering its body. Not dangerous—this applying to its danger level in the wild, it is still capable of taking a sizable piece from your finger if you get careless!

Serrasalmus serrulatus (Valenciennes, 1849)

Venezuela, Brazil. 41 cm (16 in). Not an especially colorful species, being a mixture of dull olive and silver with some dark horizontal blotches on the dorsal surface. Although very large, it is not considered to be dangerous to humans in its habitat. It is not popular in the hobby. Its status is also uncertain.

Serrasalmus spilopleura Kner, 1859
Dark banded piranha

Venezuela, Guianas, Brazil, Paraguay, Argentina. 31cm (12in). Like so many piranhas, the dark banded piranha, named for the terminal band on the caudal fin, displays sufficient variation in colors as it matures to make it difficult to describe precisely. The dorsal surface is dark, being olive green to brown. Flanks silvery. It has variable amounts of red around the throat and onto the anterior abdomen. The eyes are red. It breeds well in captivity. Regarded as being not dangerous to humans, but with sufficient doubt to be treated with great respect.

Other Genera

Species that are similar to the piranhas in other genera of Serrasalmidae are often called pacus or silver dollars. They include *Myleus*, *Metynnis*, *Mylossoma*, *Utiaritichthys*, *Acnodon*, *Mylesinus*, *Piaractus*, and *Colossoma*.

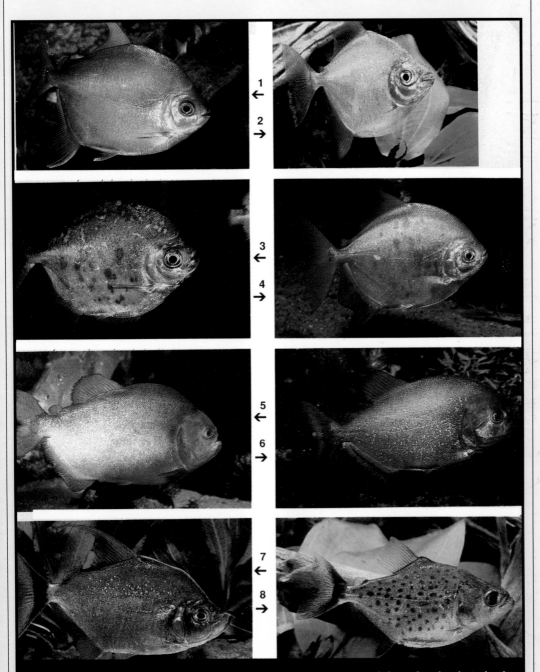

One of the ways to check your fish to ascertain whether or not it is a piranha, is to look at the distance between the end of the eye and the end of the gill cover. Piranhas always have a least two eye diameters between their eye and the end of the gill cover while the other fishes have less. 1. *Metynnis*, unidentified. 2. *Myleus rubripinnis*, a juvenile. 3. *Myleus rubripinnis* variant. 4. *Myleus rubripinnis* adult. 5. *Serrasalmus nattereri*. 6. *Serrasalmus nattereri*. 7. *Catoprion mento*. 8. *Serrasalmus hollandi*.

The black metynnis as it is sometimes called, has also passed for the black piranha. Actually it is neither. This vegetarian is *Colossoma macropomum*.

KEEPING PIRANHAS HEALTHY

Piranhas are remarkably hardy fishes in some ways, yet very delicate in others. Likewise, they are very aggressive in their nature, yet can be both exceedingly timid and nervous. For example, while they seem to recover remarkably quickly from even deep wounds, they can soon succumb to sudden drops in temperature.

They may readily become involved in battles with their own kind, or with prey, yet they can become badly stressed by excessive light, noises, and disturbances to their environment. Because they are not the most easy fishes to handle, it is altogether better that problems are avoided rather than treated.

PREVENTIVE MEDICINE

Most of the problems aquarists, indeed all pet owners, are faced with can often be traced back to a number of causes that could have been avoided by preventive husbandry techniques. These are associated with the following subjects.

1. Correct stocking levels
2. Adequate hygiene
3. Sound nutrition
4. Appreciation of stress factors
5. Prompt action when problems are detected
6. Quarantine

Without attention to these matters, all of the volumes devoted to the diseases of fishes will prove of little value, because problems will simply occur again and again. This chapter, therefore, targets these vital areas rather than cataloging diseases that are better covered in larger works where details and treatments can be explained more fully than would be possible here.

It must always be remembered that problems are rarely attributable to a single cause. Often, a combination of factors based on those listed will be present, each being contributory to the problem. Conversely, as you correct one area of management, this may directly or indirectly correct another.

STOCKING LEVELS

Lack of adequate space is a prime problem in many aquaria. Put another way, many aquarists, especially those new to the hobby, overcrowd their tanks. They assume that as long as there is sufficient oxygen to supply the needs of the fishes all will be well. Alas, this is rarely the case.

For one thing, every fish needs a given amount of space around it and adequate space in which to avoid having to be continually on the move. When this is not available the result is a build-up of tensions in the community. This dramatically increases stress and the risk of diseases resulting from this.

The communities more active state, coupled with the number of fishes, increases the carbon dioxide content, and few owners monitor this aspect. With a piranha, space is all important because these fishes are very aware of each other's destructive dental capabilities. If they are forced to coexist in a limited space the only result can be constant fighting and extreme stress.

If you ever start to think that if two are nice, three would be better, try telling yourself two may be nice, but three could be disastrous. This is likely to be the truth of the matter with piranhas unless you are prepared to invest in a much larger tank.

HYGIENE

It is really easy to introduce a pathogen (disease causing agent) into an aquarium. But it can prove almost impossible to remove it, and then only after a considerable cost has been paid in one form or another. Bacteria may gain access to the water via rocks, gravel, equipment, accessories, plants, the food, your hands, and of course via the air surrounding the tank.

You cannot avoid a degree of risk because it is inevitable, but you can minimize this by continually making sure that everything is cleaned before it is placed into the water,

and every time you take something out. Foods should be fresh and stored under cool, dark, dry conditions. Be sure to routinely clean the aquarium, removing debris and uneaten foods on a regular basis.

NUTRITION

A varied and balanced diet is the cornerstone of good health. If you start to take short cuts in the quality or quantity of food you offer your piranhas, you are heading on a downhill path that can only increase the risk of illness. With piranhas there is the added factor that if two or more fish are living together, any shortfall in their diet will invariably result in an increased rate of aggression, and maybe the eating of the smaller or weaker individual(s) by the larger, stronger ones.

This being said, you must make sure that the food supplied is eaten, otherwise it will create another problem, that of polluting the water with its own attendant problems.

THE STRESS FACTOR

Stress is a major ballplayer in the causes of diseases. It reduces the immune system's ability to function at full capacity, thus it lowers resistance to even the most insignificant of ailments. The problem of identifying stress factors is that they are not always the same for each animal—what upsets one may not do so to the next.

However, as a general guide it can be assumed that the more natural the action that is denied the animal, the greater the stress factor. Piranhas always have adequate space in the wild, so lack of it will cause stress. They are able to keep given distances from each other in the wild. If this is not possible in your aquarium, this too will be a major stress factor.

They are nervous, indeed timid, fishes that have lots of hiding places in the wild, so should have similar hiding places in an aquarium. They can easily avoid bright sunshine in the wild, so should not be

A school of piranhas lives in peace in a large aquarium providing they are always well fed.

Serrasalmus nattereri spawning.

subjected to it in the aquarium—or should have ample shaded places where they can avoid it. No fishes like light entering from the sides of their environment—it makes them nervous. You should thus screen the back and sides of their aquarium which at least limits the laterally entering light to the front viewing glass.

Avoid sudden noises and sudden changes in light intensities. Be sure that in a community situation the fishes are all of the same size. If not, the smaller ones will be badly stressed by the closeness of larger, potentially predatory conspecifics. Try to avoid free-for-all feeding techniques—feed each piranha its own meal at opposite ends of the aquarium so as to avoid confrontation or bullying.

PROMPT ACTION TO PROBLEMS

If you suspect one of your fish is ill, do not wait to see how things develop over the next few days. Chances are high that they will simply get much worse. The fish must either be treated in the aquarium, or it must be removed for individual treatment in a hospital tank. An added problem with piranhas is that if one of a small community of these fishes becomes ill it is less able to avoid attacks by its fellows and may suffer badly as a result.

Make notes on any problems, both clinical signs and those that are behavioral, then seek advice as quickly as possible. The sooner treatment is effected, the sooner a recovery will be made. Remember, if medicines are to be added to the main tank, you must remove carbon and other filter materials that might adsorb them. Also, you may have to slow down the filter flow rate to allow the medicines more time to work.

The down side of this is that it may adversely effect the beneficial bacterial colony in the substrate, so only slow things down for short periods. This fact also underscores the benefit of never overcrowding an aquarium, thus placing a heavy strain on the filter system. Check to see whether or not the medicine is "friendly" to substrate bacteria.

In a failed breeding attempt, this *Serrasalmus spilopleura* lost parts of its fins. Usually such problems resolve themselves without medication or treatment. But if they fungus, immediate action must be taken to save the life of the fish.

Serrasalmus gibbus is a magnificent fish and is very dangerous both in nature and in the tank. It is, however, very sensitive to medicines and chemicals put into the aquarium water. If one becomes ill, treat it in a separate tank.

QUARANTINE

Once you have an established aquarium, a golden rule should be that no additional stock is introduced to this unless it has passed through a quarantine period to minimize the risk of introducing pathogens into the tank.

This means that you must have a spare tank, albeit a smaller one, in which new arrivals can spend 14-21 days while you check them out. This tank can double as a hospital tank. When setting up a quarantine tank, the water should be adjusted to the water temperature and chemistry of the seller's tank. It can then be adjusted over the quarantine period to match that of your display aquarium.

While the new arrivals are in quarantine you can observe their eating habits and adjust these to your own regimen. As a general precaution against parasites, it is recommended that you add about one teaspoonful of salt per gallon of water. A good hand lens would also be worthwhile so that you could carefully study your new pet to check to see that it is free of any obvious external parasites. Furnish the tank sparsely, but include some places it can retreat to. Use plastic rather than real plants, and dark glass marbles can be used as a substrate. A simple filter, and possibly an air stone, should ensure adequate filtration and aeration.

RECOGNIZING A SICK PIRANHA

A fish will either show behavioral, clinical, or no signs of ill health. Those that show no signs of a problem of course are impossible to treat because the first you know of a problem is when you find a dead piranha, or its remains if it has been partly devoured. The latter is worse because if it was ill, and was then eaten, the pathogen may have been transported to a new host.

Behavioral Signs: The fish will be listless, may hide far more than is normal, may make darting movements through the tank, may be seen rubbing against rocks, gasping at the surface, swimming at an unusual angle, show disinterest in its food, or lay on the substrate with its fins clamped close to its body or fully extended.

Clinical Signs: Any swellings or lumps; cloudiness of the eyes; cottonwool like

The most rare and most elegant of the piranhas is the black piranha, *Serrasalmus niger* from Brazil.

growths anywhere on the head, body, or fins; white, yellow, black, or other spots (other than those which are features of the species); rotting fins that are streaked with blood, undue swelling of the abdomen; blood streaked fecal matter; bulging or sunken eyes; emaciation; holes anywhere on the fish; scales standing away from the body; excessive mucus on the skin resulting in a dulling of the colors; ulcers; gray color to the gills (instead of a healthy pink), or inflammation of these.

Wounds and missing parts of fins are quite common in piranhas, given their lifestyle, but ordinarily these will not cause too much of a problem, and they regenerate quite quickly. However, the danger here is that they can be the site for parasitic or bacterial invasion, which in turn can lead to a secondary infection. This is far more likely if the water is not clean and of the required quality and temperature.

PHOTO BY DR. HERBERT R. AXELROD.

These piranhas were collected in the Rio Aguaro, Venezuela by Dr. Axelrod. They were identified as *Serrasalmus hollandi* by Dr. Gery and as *Pygocentrus striolatus* by Dr. Fernandez-Yepez.

TREATMENTS

For many minor problems a raising of the temperature by a few degrees may be effective, as might the addition of salt to the water (as mentioned), and possibly at a higher concentration—2-3 teaspoonfuls per gallon. Other treatments will utilize any of numerous modern drugs that have been produced for tropical fishes in recent years.

However, before using these medicines it is important that you are sure what you are treating, otherwise the medicine will not be effective: it may even aggravate the situation! Veterinary advice—or that of an experienced aquarist or well established dealer—is therefore suggested.

If, following a treatment, the problem recurs, the chances are high that conditions in the aquarium are not satisfactory. Alternatively, the spores of some pathogens are very resilient to treatments.

The solution may be a total breaking down of the aquarium, the destruction of the plants, the replacement of the rocks, or a heavy disinfecting of these with household bleach, and careful cleaning of the filter system and everything else that is in contact with the water. Such action is, fortunately, not often needed, but the thought of having to do this should prompt all aquarists to pay that extra attention to general husbandry techniques.

Finally, it should be added that when purchasing fishes it really does pay to carefully check the tanks of those selling the fishes to ensure that their standards of management are of the highest order. Do not go for the cheapest fishes because a dealer who invests the time and money in maintaining high standards simply cannot compete with merchants who are able to cut prices simply because they have poor standards of care and nutrition.